The Vocabulary of Joy

The Vocabulary of Joy

Celebrating the Blessings of Life with Cancer

Julie Savage Parker

Handwoven Webs Press
Asheville, North Carolina

The Vocabulary of Joy
Celebrating the Blessings of Life with Cancer

Julie Savage Parker

Published by:
Handwoven Webs Press
1 Battle Square Suite 909
Asheville NC 28801

handwovenwebs.com
info@handwovenwebs.com

A special thanks to Alla Renee Bozarth for generously allowing me to include *Bakerwoman God* and to Judyth Hill for generously allowing me to include *Wage Peace*

Cover and Interior Design: Julie Savage Parker

DEDICATION
With deepest gratitude to
Lisa Lichtig, MD,
Brian Ritchie Lewis, MD,
and Diane Douglas, OT
for their loving kindness and
their profound roles in my Healing.

*"I can no other answer make but thanks,
And thanks; and ever thanks."*

Twelfth Night Act III Scene 3, William Shakespeare

CONTENTS

"…whatever the complaint is, it's always the same thing: something beneficial trying to happen. In true medicine there is no conflict, no enemy, no disease, only the opportunity to bring someone out of the dream of strife into the dream of wholeness."
Eliot Cowan, *Plant Spirit Medicine*

INTRODUCTION

Welcome to my shores! If you have landed here, you may be dancing with cancer yourself. I confess I was quite surprised to have been diagnosed with cancer in 2013. Cancer is not something I had ever feared or really given much thought to at all prior to my doctor telling me I had won the dubious lottery and had it myself. But now I have it (or had it?) and I am learning so much about myself and about life and healing. I thought you might want to look at cancer through my eyes for a bit.

I have been surrounded by so many people who have contributed to my healing in their own unique ways. The latest to arrive on my shores was Whitman Bolles who came on board as my editor and proceeded to poke and prod me to dig deeper and turn over rocks to reveal the fertile soil beneath. I decided to make him quite visible in the book, especially when I want to blame him for something, as in "Whitman made me do it!" or sometimes "Whitman wouldn't let me do it!" as in banning me from using a combination question mark and exclamation point (as in 'OMG, really?!'). There are none left in the book, alas.

You will see Whitman crop up from time to time so don't be alarmed when he does. He has not only made this book much richer, but in doing so, he has made my healing more complete.

When you have finished the book, if you email me at julie@ handwovenwebs.com, I will email a link to the "living" book that is the companion to *The Vocabulary of Joy*. where you will find links to the articles and websites mentioned here and to further writing. And maybe we can start a conversation about healing...

PREFACE

The Vocabulary of Joy is about my journey and mine alone. My dance with cancer may be unlike anyone else's, but it is my hope that at least some aspects of my journey may prove helpful to others. While I feel in my gut (and my head, and my heart) that what I have written is valid, it is not my intent to *prove* the validity of what I am saying to the skeptical reader. Take what you will and leave the rest.

Please do not assume that the ideas put forth here are necessarily shared by any of the doctors you'll find on these pages. Some ideas may be, others may not. My feelings, beliefs, and attitudes come from deep within me and have been crystallized by my own dance with cancer. I have dotted the i's and crossed the t's of my belief system with my own readings on cancer and healing and I have been amply blessed by angels around me. It feels like while I am running the marathon, the road is lined with people thrusting water my way and cheering me on. I am doing the running, but their loving support gets me across the finish line.

Julie Savage Parker
Summer 2016
Asheville NC

In Which My World is NOT Turned Upside Down

"For a seed to achieve its greatest expression,
it must come completely undone.
The shell cracks, its insides come out and everything changes.
To someone who doesn't understand growth,
it would look like complete destruction."
Cynthia Occelli

Or maybe my world was turned upside down, but not in the way you might expect. In late September of 2013 I was told I had ovarian cancer. A few days later, a surgeon removed my ovaries, Fallopian tubes, uterus, and for good measure—my appendix. Oh and they drained three and a half liters of fluid (*ascites* if you are already cancer-literate) that had been floating around in my belly. (Can you imagine carrying around that much fluid in your belly?) I spent almost a week in the hospital while they were searching for the 'primary' cancer. To this day I am not certain why they assumed this was secondary and there was a primary cancer lurking somewhere in my body, but at any rate they never found it. Eventually they sent a piece of me to Johns Hopkins where even the cream of the medical crop was at a loss. But the medical details of my cancer journey are really insignificant. What matters more, much more, is my journey of the mind and spirit. The body came along for the ride, and of course was the prime mover of the journey, but really I think it was only a catalyst for my transformation.

Now I should tell you—right here in the second paragraph—I have no medical training whatsoever. I have no expertise at all. I just had cancer. But my oncologist has not had cancer, nor has my primary care doctor had cancer, so they can only observe cancer from a safe distance—through a microscope as it were, while my body/mind/spirit danced with cancer in a way they will never fully understand. I wore it to bed at night, I woke up with it, I showered with it, I ate breakfast, lunch, and dinner with it.

Also right here at the beginning I should make it clear why I am writing this book, but the truth is, I just know I need to write it. The *why* of it is unraveling as I write. You see, I have never even heard of anyone having this sort of dance with cancer. I typically hear that their world was 'torn apart', 'turned upside down' or that they were 'devastated'. I obviously dance to the beat of my own drum as none of that happened to me! If my experience is so very different from other peoples' experience, how can it be helpful to others? My story may sound like a fairy tale to the rest of the world, or perhaps science fiction. But it did happen and it is not fiction of any kind, so I beg the reader's indulgence while I speculate about the nature of illness—or my illness anyway. I will consider illness as metaphor and whether I asked for this illness in any way. I will muse about how it has served me, how it is moving me from chrysalis to butterfly, helping me spread my wings and fly. And along the way I learned a thing or two about healing cancer, and I will share what I learned that might be of help to others on this journey.

LET ME BE CLEAR: this is about my very personal journey with cancer. It may generalize to other people or it may not. I am not out to say this is the way you should feel, this is how you should respond, but I would like to tap you on the shoulder and invite you perhaps not to automatically buy into the panic, not to swallow the party line, and even not to automatically assume that the "standard of care" is your best option. It may indeed be more harmful than helpful, and sometimes even causes irreparable damage. In fact, it is the "standard of care" that scares me, not the cancer itself.

What is most strange—most like science fiction—is that when I was told I had cancer, I felt no fear. Or if I explore my psyche deeply enough, I think at that point what I feared most was *life*. A few years prior to my diagnosis, my life shattered into tiny little pieces. Pretty much every aspect of my life went spinning out of control. My work—what paid the bills (just barely)—dried up with the economy. When that happened, after eight years of living in the same house, I began to be late paying the rent every month, and eventually my landlord decided that it was time I skedaddle. I had three dogs and no money to find us all another roof. Before I could find us a place to live, my beloved (healthy, young) dog Charley up and died… and my dear Freya, who was 18, had to be put to sleep.

I considered, for a while, moving into my car with my third dog— my sweet Anna. In the summer. I actually looked for trees under which I could park. Then my blood pressure shot up to 280/160 and they whisked me to the hospital. Turns out I may have something called cerebral amyloid angiopathy (CAA), which means my brain is bleeding. The neurologist told me it was congenital and untreatable. Google told me I could go from a normal brain to advanced dementia in one week. A fine how-do-you-do, no? It was scary, and for months I asked a couple of close friends to let me know if they saw signs of dementia. I wondered what actions a person might need to take if that happened. Suppose it started on a Sunday—how do I prepare for Friday if I had one week left of a functioning brain? What do I do? Where do I go? Do I call all my friends and say "goodbye"? After about six months I began to relax a bit. I figured as long as "cerebral amyloid angiopathy" still rolled off my tongue, I was probably okay. It is six years later and I can still say it, and the only sign of CAA is that I now need a walker.

But none of this compares with the devastation I felt when I lost my Work—the thing that brought me joy, that was a superb outlet for creativity in so many areas, the Work that I felt was my *dharma*, my *raison d'être*. In 2002 I began a regional magazine for women whose tag-line was *Celebrating the Strength, Wisdom, and Grace of Women*. It was my passion to have a platform—to 'hold space for'—women to come forth and, in a sense, sit around the fire with each other, to contribute their stories, their wisdom. *I wanted to encourage women to find wisdom within themselves.* I had lost patience with magazines where someone was always set apart as an expert on a topic, and who pontificated to the crowd gathered at their feet. I'd also lost patience with stories short enough to appease the attention span of a gnat. I wanted stories that honored the *everywoman*, not just the 'celebrities' in the community, and a publication that reflected the essence of those women who found themselves drawn to this area. I wanted a publication whose contents would not be in the typical women's publication. In fact, we used as an example not wanting an article on 'preparing for cold and flu season' because—good grief—that is not woman specific, not region specific, and appears in almost every other magazine on the planet, year after year.

I also wanted a place for *celebration*, a place to applaud the best in life (not to bemoan the worst)—a safe place, where a woman would know the contents would make her sit a bit taller and smile a bit more broadly, and feel more powerful, rather than feel more frightened, more defeated, more angry. The magazine was a place where our attention could be on what we want in life, not what we don't want. All of these issues were very important to me, and a source of great satisfaction to bring that to the forefront. I felt so honored to hold that space for women. While I was doing that work, sometimes I felt the whole Universe was carrying me forward in a great, powerful, joyful wave of energy.

We sprinkled the magazine with quotations from women, women being so often overlooked in the public discourse. We also

The Vocabulary of Joy

honored men once a year (and of course in that issue, all the quotations were by men). And I loved highlighting a wide variety of women's voices rather than the same voices month after month in the columns or departments of the typical rag mag. And I loved designing the covers and the monthly themes, and, and, and... The whole process was a total joy, and I connected with lots of people in the process. As a publisher, I could call people up and ask to interview them, and as a typically rather shy person, it was so great to have a magazine behind me. I felt so very, very blessed to do that work, and to offer the opportunity to a wide variety of women to speak through the publication. I felt my whole life had prepared me for that work and it was so delicious to be able to do work I loved while making a contribution to the world. I felt so very fortunate to be in that position.

When, after eight years, the woman with whom I was doing the publication no longer shared that vision, the partnership was no longer viable, and I left.

When that happened, I actually felt my creative center had been ripped out of my body. I no longer had a voice, I no longer had a creative outlet, I no longer had contact with so many wonderful people. And then my "head exploded" when my blood pressure shot up to 280/160 with the rage and the grief and the enormity of the loss. And a few short years later, my creative center was literally, rather than just metaphorically, ripped out of my body with the hysterectomy—the first sign of illness as metaphor. First my body corroded with the anger and grief and loss and sense of betrayal that ate me alive—literally—and then the surgeon finished the job. Is it any wonder I feared life more than I feared death? I actually welcomed the cancer for a moment as a way out of living past so much loss. I see a direct correspondence between these emotional losses and the loss of a good chunk of my body. And now that I think about it, my world turning upside down is what preceded, not followed, a diagnosis of cancer. I have since learned that it is not at all uncommon for cancer to follow a major loss or trauma. I ultimately discovered, though, that the cancer did not turn my life upside down—it turned it *rightside up*!

Once my ovaries, Fallopian tubes, and uterus were cut out of my body, it began to feel a bit like a relief, like a suppurating, festering sore had been excised, drained, and made ready to begin its healing journey, starting with the food I put in my mouth. The minute I got home from the hospital I started googling cancer and healing, cancer and herbs, cancer and vitamins, cancer and nutrition, cancer and essential oils, etc. (If I'd had a computer in the hospital, I probably would have started googling the minute they wheeled me out of surgery.) Any pairing of cancer and alternative, integrative, holistic and my ears perked up. It was immediately clear to me that I had to put what knowledge I already had about healthy eating into action, and to build on that knowledge in as many ways as possible. And I had something positive to focus on, something over which I had control: my healing journey from cancer. Yes, I mean *positive*. A diagnosis of cancer has clearly been a gift for me.

I invite you to consider a radically different approach to cancer.

"When you come to the end of your rope,
tie a knot and hang on."
Franklin D. Roosevelt

In Which I Contemplate the "C" Word

Cancer sucks! Fuck cancer! That seems to be the language and the attitude of many people with cancer, but I suggest it may not be so much the cancer itself that sucks, but the *conventional treatment* of cancer that drains the life out of the human body and even perhaps the human spirit. The problem is, too many people assume that conventional treatment is their only choice, wthat cancer and its typical treatment are inseparable.

Cancer is sometimes called the "C" word, as if the word itself is too terrible to speak. Think Voldemort (He-Who-Must-Not-Be-Named). *Voll* in German is full and *mort* in French is death. Cancer is indeed too often seen as 'full of death', and with conventional treatment, that is not just perception, but too often reality.

When he learned I planned to write about the "C" word, Whitman reminded me of the other "C" word (referring to female genitalia)—certainly one of the most heavily tabooed of all English words. *Once an ancient title of respect for women*, there is a decades old movement by feminists to reclaim the word. Think about it: *cunt* actually represents the source of life. [If this is just all too shocking for you, take a look at cherishthecunt.com for a fascinating historical look at the word and you'll beam with pride if you happen to have one of your own.]

In a similar way, I have reclaimed "cancer" as a rite of passage, one that set me on a s/hero's journey to becoming whole. For me, "cancer" became a source of *life*, not a source of death. But whether we call it the "C" word or "the Big C" or simply "cancer", I suggest we divest the word of its power to strike terror in the hearts of mere mortals. We gave the word its power, and we can take it away.

I have come face to face with Voldemort (in the guise of cancer) but I flipped the script and changed fairy tales: I decided was actually in OZ. Toto and I pulled back the screen only to find that the fierce Wizard of Cancer was not at all what he seemed.

MAKING MY CHOICE
I have always known that if I were ever faced with cancer, I would decline conventional treatment, without question. When talking with people without cancer, they typically say while they'd really prefer to heal naturally, when actually faced with cancer, they were not 100% certain they'd stick with that decision. Well, I was and am so very comfortable with the decision—healing cancer naturally for me is like falling softly and safely into a mother's arms.

Now that I think about it, that is exactly what it is... into the arms of Mother Earth and Mother Nature. What better source of solace and healing? And if I was not already in the arms of these two Mamas, cancer served as a blessing to scoot me in that direction.

There are three people who have helped me find my way. It strikes me as I am writing this that, without hyperbole, I probably owe them my life. First and foremost is Lisa Lichtig, my Plant Spirit Medicine healer. Lisa is a shaman—and she is also an MD. (Let's see, should I call her Glenda the Good Witch?)

To give you a glimpse of Lisa, between medical school and her residency she spent a year in Nigeria, West Africa as an international health fellow. "I was gifted with a deeper experience of the relevance of human friendships and how essential community is for sustaining life. I also met the Sun, the Earth, the Moon and Water in a new way."

Who better to guide me in my own journey to meeting the Sun, the Earth, the Moon and the Water?

Lisa studied imagery and healing with Dr. Norman Cousins and Dr. O. Carl Simonton, both pioneers in these fields. She studied too with the renowned Dr. Tieroana Lowdog and became a clinical herbalist under her guidance. At the turn of the century, she began an intensive 15-year apprenticeship to become a mara'akame (medicine person) in the Huichol lineage under the guidance of Tsauirrikame Eliot Cowan. From Lisa: "*I offer individual healing sessions to people who long for reconnection, balance and alleviation of suffering in their lives. Traditional shamanic healing sets things into motion to bring about balance. I also call upon plant spirit medicine in my healing work to support the natural flow of energy and emotion which support balance. In addition to individual healing sessions, I periodically am called upon to work with rituals and ceremonies that guide community to reconnect with the living, singing world throughout the various stages of life.*"

Balance! Fundamentally, I am seeking balance, I realized. I have shifted out of balance and harmony within myself and with the world, and I need a guide to help me re-balance. Lisa Lichtig has been, for me, that guide. Plant Spirit Medicine has been my primary cancer treatment—my own, best, quintessential "chemo".

I have totally re-framed my life. While "natural" has always been my preference, now I make even more mindful choices, not out of fear or desperation, but with the ahhhh attitude of falling into Mama's arms. Luckily I have always been repelled by things like nail polish and hair dye so I have not poisoned my body with them. I have used very little makeup in my life. I have not put things on my body that are typically toxic. I have had antibiotics maybe once. I have no pills for headaches or stomach aches or any of the typical over-the-counter remedies in my medicine cabinet.

So why did I get cancer, you ask. Well, my downfall has been convenience food, uh, fast food, (so embarrassing to admit) and my nemesis—Pepsi. Lord have mercy, how much better off I would be without soda! I have known that for years, but lordy did it taste good. From time to time, I even tried very mindfully drinking sodas, really wrapping my tongue around the flavor, trying to figure out what was so appealing. But that was a tricky one as sometimes I could not figure out what I ever saw in it, and other times it was practically the nectar of the gods. Go figure.

As I write this, I remembered why Pepsi is "mother's milk" to me! When I was a baby, there were only glass baby bottles, and apparently I tended to throw mine and they'd break. Eventually my mother said "Enough of that!" and she started affixing nipples to Pepsi bottles, being much cheaper to replace, should I wind up my pitching arm again. What do you know... I wonder if there is really a connection there?

Twice in the past 4 years I ate only bologna sandwiches. (I can see your look of horror...) I had so little money, I thought that might be the cheapest meal I could come up with. So for a while it was bologna sandwiches, breakfast, lunch, and dinner. And no, it was not tofu bologna—it was the real thing, made out of highly processed animals that were not treated kindly. I had a side of shame with each bite.

In re-framing, re-designing my life, I have (sometimes radically) altered (1) what I put in my body, (2) what I put on my body, and (3) what I put around my body, in my environment.

In *In Which My Fork Leads the Way*, I will go into more detail on what I put in my body. I will give you an overview and references for a cancer diet. (HINT: No sugar, no sugar, no sugar!) Much of what I put in my body was inspired by the second person to whom I owe my life, or at the very least, whatever burgeoning wellness I am managing to cultivate, and that is Dr. Brian Ritchie Lewis. You can read about Dr. Lewis in his doctor hat (or should I say, with his stethoscope neck) in *In Which I Deal With My Doctors*, and you can read about his alter ego, Brian Lewis, qigong teacher, in *In Which I Begin to Move*.

The third person to whom this book is dedicated is my dear friend Diane Douglas. Diane (as you will see) had a major role in helping me through the onset of cancer. As much as I value that, what has touched the most is—her touch! The work I am doing with her has been life-altering, no exaggeration. Diane does something called Integrative Manual Therapy, plus whatever other magic she has in her hip pocket. She can feel if the ankle bone is talking to the thighbone, the thigh bone is talking to... well, you get the idea. She can feel what is going on in there and she helps all the pieces talk with each other, helps the information flow where it should. When she is doing cranio-sacral therapy, I swear she is vibrating her fingers on my head...but it is me! It is me, waking up inside, dancing and flowing and all coming alive.

These three beautiful people and so many others have walked by my side on my road to healing.

So, I invite you to join me in my journey of exploring the "Big C" or the "C" word or cancer or whatever you choose to call it and see how together we might "flip the script" on the journey.

In Which I Make Love, Not War

"When we focus on waging a war or fighting a battle versus healing our lives and bodies we are interfering with the healing process."
Bernie Siegal

A quick google search for "battling cancer" netted 51,900,000 results. Fifty-one MILLION, nine hundred thousand. War is the dominant paradigm for encounters with cancer. No wonder so many people are dying on the "battlefield"! There is even a non-profit called "Cancer Crackdown" whose tag line is "Fighting Together" and all people with cancer are called "fighters". The site is littered with the words "fight" and "battle". I can't imagine waking up every morning with my first thoughts that I am at war with my own body, that I have an enemy inside me. That is the stuff of nightmares! I think these folks, while certainly well-intentioned, are doing people with cancer a huge disservice to couch the cancer journey in those terms. Stirring up people's fight or flight response—waging war—I feel is the worst possible way to regain balance and harmony. Perhaps some people feel that fighting is the only way to accomplish their goal—to make the cancer go away—by killing the cancer. Peace is much more likely to provide the healing balm for body and soul.

I have been reading about cancer and language, and while there is a growing distaste for such language, the main objection is that

The Vocabulary of Joy

In Which I Make Love, Not War

it might make those who are obviously 'losing the battle' feel bad about themselves. What concerns me is that "fightin' words" put us in opposition to our own flesh. I choose to work *with* my body, not in opposition to it.

This is a mindset that too often pervades the public consciousness. The moment we declare an enemy of any sort, the moment we *declare war*, it energizes our opponent and forces the other side to 'gird their loins' and enter into battle. We are much better off avoiding the loin girding and engaging in a partnership with our bodies—negotiating, looking for common ground, working together to move forward. [The same with politicians—I so don't want to vote for anyone who vows to 'fight' for me.]

And what happens with the influx of cortisol (known as the stress hormone) when people insist on using "fight", "battle", "war", etc. Everytime they say "this terrible/horrible disease", "this devastating disease", everytime they talk about their life being "turned upside down", surely that shoots cortisol through the veins of the newly diagnosed reading those words as well as through their own veins.

"War is a mind-set, and all action that comes out of such a mind-set will either strengthen the enemy, the perceived evil, or, if the war is won, will create a new enemy, a new evil equal to and often worse than the one that was defeated. There is a deep interrelatedness between your state of consciousness and external reality... Whatever you fight, you strengthen, and what you resist, persists."
Eckhart Tolle

"There is a mania in our society, the manic physical energy and how much a part of the war on cancer that has become. Exercise, ostensibly a healthy thing, can literally wear people out (look at all the triathlons and marathons being run by cancer patients/ survivors—as if they are proving they've won the battle), and the constant motion, the constant searching for something on the

material plane only serves as an excuse for completely ignoring
one's feelings, not ever sitting still, listening, observing. And as we
know, suppressing emotion and illness go hand in hand."
Whitman Bolles

Posted online from another person dancing with cancer who says
it beautifully:

> *"I never felt that I should go to war and fight to survive. I*
> *thought it was better to become friends with cancer. I wasn't*
> *afraid of dying, nor angry about this sudden turn of events.*
> *I was at peace with the prospect of moving on, even though*
> *there were still things I wanted to do, like teach what I had*
> *learned about authentic living and speaking truthfully. Still,*
> *I felt that death was not my enemy; after all, it has been*
> *with me from the first moment of my existence. I know I*
> *disappointed many people when I told them I had made*
> *death my friend and that I wasn't going to start a war against*
> *cancer."*
> *Posted on Thursday, 21 January 2016 Robert Rabbin*

Speaking of language, I dislike the term "survivor"—too much like
war. I dislike "surthriver"—too cutesy. I very very much dislike
"victim" of cancer. What *do* I propose? I am still working on that
one.

In Rachel Naomi Remen, MD's book *Kitchen Table Wisdom*, on
page 169-170 she tells a story I want to share with you (better yet,
go buy the book and turn to page 169!). She speaks of her family
putting together a large jigsaw puzzle over a period of time. As
a very young girl, she found the darker pieces scary, and she'd
sneak into the living room and hide the "bad" ones. Eventually her
mother found out about the hidden pieces, little Naomi returned
them, and the family completed the puzzle which, when all the
pieces were in place (both dark and light) was a scene of stunning
beauty.

Sometimes we find dark pieces in the jigsaw of our life and we want to destroy them. But if we accept them and love them all into place, I believe our life too can become a scene of stunning beauty.

MIND BODY SPIRIT
Recently I came across the term biopsychosocial (BPS) medicine, sometimes biopsychosocial / spirit medicine. Is this the allopathic world's way of saying mind/body/spirit medicine? My dance with cancer (not battle—dance!) finds me do-se-do-ing in each of these areas. And throughout it all, I am LOVING my cancer back into balance! I have warned my friends that I will haunt them if, when I die (should I die of cancer), they say "Julie lost her battle with cancer". Nor do I want anyone to say "That Julie, she was a fighter!" Beyond the banality of the cliché, it is the attitude that breaks my heart. Let's be lovers, not fighters. What an appalling idea to declare war on anything under our own skin! Our bodies work so hard for us doing literally billions of things every second of every day. A human body is nothing less than an engineering marvel. Cancer has revealed its beauty more than its brokenness. If our body is out of balance, we need not declare war on it or on any part of it. We absolutely must love ourselves back to health. Let's see: besides cancer, we have declared war on hunger, on poverty, on drugs, and on terror—how's that working out for us?

Isaac Chan in *Words matter: cancer and 'fighting' language* tells us: *"Cancer is a unique disease. To take the war analogy further, cancer is not a foreign agent infiltrating our bodies, such as an infection — cancer is a coup d'état, a tumorous growth from within us. One of the great paradoxes of cancer treatment is that targeting cancer inevitably means targeting our own bodies.*

"Yet because we conflate cancer and conflict, physicians and patients often find themselves in the midst of an unintentional civil war, fighting for life to the very end. We have inadvertently created a culture where death is considered a failure, and life

extension equals life."

In The Guardian, in *Having cancer is not a fight or a battle,* Kate Granger says, *"Why is military language used to describe cancer? These words are meant to help patients but can have the opposite effect. 'She lost her brave fight.' If anyone mutters those words after my death, wherever I am, I will curse them.*

"... the language used around cancer seems to revolve around wartime rhetoric: battle, fight, warrior, beat. While I recognise that these violent words may help others on their journey with cancer, as someone who is never going to 'win her battle' with this disease, I find them uncomfortable and frustrating to hear.

"... I live with it and I let its physical and emotional effects wash over me. But I don't fight it. After all, cancer has arisen from within my own body, from my own cells. To fight it would be 'waging a war' on myself."

NOTE: These articles and more will be linked in the living book companion to this book. Email me at julie@handwovenwebs.com and I will send you a link to the living book.

I offer this poem with profound gratitude to Judyth Hill for allowing me to share her beautiful work. (Note the date.)

WAGE PEACE

Wage peace with your breath.

Breathe in firemen and rubble,
breathe out whole buildings and flocks of red wing blackbirds.

Breathe in terrorists
and breathe out sleeping children and freshly mown fields.

The Vocabulary of Joy

In Which I Make Love, Not War

Breathe in confusion and breathe out maple trees.
Breathe in the fallen and breathe out lifelong friendships intact.

Wage peace with your listening: hearing sirens, pray loud.

Remember your tools: flower seeds, clothes pins, clean rivers.

Make soup.

Play music, memorize the words for thank you in three languages.

Learn to knit, and make a hat.

Think of chaos as dancing raspberries,
imagine grief
as the outbreath of beauty
or the gesture of fish

Swim for the other side.

Wage peace.

Never has the world seemed so fresh and precious:

Have a cup of tea …and rejoice.
Act as if armistice has already arrived.
Celebrate today.

Judyth Hill ~ September 11, 2001

If you have a cancer diagnosis, with this book I want to inspire you
to breathe in cancer and breathe out harmony; breathe in fear and
breathe out peace; Have a cup of tea and rejoice. Act as if *healing*
has already arrived.

WORDS FROM WHITMAN:
Whitman keeps urging me to put the emails I send him right in the book. Well Whitman, what's sauce for the goose... What you keep contributing to the unfolding of this book is so rich, now I'm putting YOUR email directly in the book!

> *"What you're implying but don't quite state is the FEAR necessary to wage this war. Can't have a war without an army, and can't have an army without a bunch of extremely fearful soldiers. Also, as we discussed, the poem is a Western poetic version of traditional Tibetan tonglen meditation, and Pema Chodron among others has written a lot about using this technique in dealing with illness. Maybe also acknowledge how this idea (letting go of control) runs so counter to everything we are taught in this society, so it will doubtless be difficult for many, at first, but once a person experiences the results, then the discussion is no longer abstract. After all, this whole transformation that you're modeling is one that must be experienced; that's the only way it exists."*

> *"I know two patients who tired of their therapy, went home with extensive cancer and 'Left their troubles to God.' And their cancers disappeared. No wars—just peace."*
> Bernie Siegal

In Which I Whine and Curse the Fates A Bit

"Just when it looks like life is falling apart, it may be falling together for the first time. I have learned to trust the process of life, and not so much the outcome. Destinations have not nearly as much value as journeys. So maybe you should let things fall apart at this juncture if that's what's happening. Don't hang on so tenaciously. The nice thing about things falling apart is that you can pick up only the pieces that you want."
Neale Donald Walsh

Well, you may be thinking this woman is way too much tra la la, way too much Pollyanna for my taste. She's being awfully sanguine about having cancer— twice! So here is a chapter to provide some balance.

GDFSE

GDFSE! That is a string of curse words, not fit for family consumption. It comes from my college days and has its own back-story (perhaps another book one day?) but sometimes I feel like cursing the fates. Since my life fell apart in 2010 (the year from hell) when I was banished from Mars Hill and began my nomad's journey about Western North Carolina, I lived in Marshall (1 month), Candler (5 days), Weaverville (1 month), Asheville (1 year), Leicester (1 year), Hendersonville (10 months), Asheville (5 days, 3 of which were in the hospital), Mars Hill again (1 month),

Black Mountain (5 days) Fairview (11 months), Asheville (8 months), West Asheville (6 months), until finally coming to rest here where I will likely live the rest of my life. While the Pollyanna in me trusts this was all part of a Divine Plan for my ultimate well-being, another part of me (let's call her Morticia) is totally exhausted from struggling to keep a roof over my head and at least twice making preparations to move into my car. Did you count? That is 14 different roofs in 6 years. All except the last two roofs, with my dear dog Anna by my side. What a trooper she was, having her world change so drastically again and again. Hmm... what a trooper *I* was!

All of this on top of having my losing my Work (GDFSE, GDFSE!!! —another backstory, one I choose to omit), the deaths of all three of my dogs, two stays in the hospital before either cancer (one for a bleeding brain and one for a nasty attack of gout) and one for undiagnosed belly pain a few months ago. They say the top five stressful life events are: death of a loved one (3 of them), divorce, moving (14 times), major illness (3 of them), and job loss. The only one of the bunch I missed was divorce, though actually loss of a business along with a business partner bore a strong resemblance to a divorce. GDFSE! Hiccup, whimper. Sigh...

Well, I was worn out, and I am somewhat recovered at this point, but no wonder my body reacted with two cancers. Oh, and the five-day stay in Asheville? I had just moved in to a new place and been there maybe a day and a half (not at all unpacked) when gout raged and sent me to the hospital. On the day before I was hospitalized, Anna had an 'accident' in the house (actually, I am pretty sure it was deliberate because she knew that was the wrong roof for us) and my housemate told me we had to move. I did understand her position, but while I was in the hospital (friends had come and rescued Anna) I learned through the grapevine (she did not even have the good grace to tell me) she had moved all of my furniture to the basement, so there I was in the hospital, (did I mention I was in the hospital?) in significant pain, finding out I had nowhere to live when I got out. As I write this, my chest has tightened and my breathing has slowed to a crawl.

Oh, and another tale/tail of woe: while I was in the hospital for the hysterectomy, my beloved dog Anna freaked out. My two dear friends with whom I shared a house were taking care of her in my absence, but Anna wasn't having it. She constantly paced and whined and was generally beside herself. Her distress became so severe, it occurred to me I might have to have her put to sleep—in my absence!

That tore me apart, fearing (1) the death of my beloved dog (2) how awful for someone else to have to take her to her last trip to the vet (she has always been terrified of vets) (3) how betrayed and frightened Anna would feel (4) how damn helpless I felt, lying sliced up in the hospital, 6 missing organs, still catheterized, on oxygen, and not even able to get out of bed yet.

So, the previous time in the hospital I learned I had nowhere to live and had to quickly—from my hospital bed—find a roof for our heads, and this time in the hospital face possibly putting my dog to sleep. Sh*t. GDF(S)E.

Anna finally settled down somewhat so we did not have to put her to sleep. She got a reprieve, though as she had started having seizures and then regular household accidents, the woman I was later living with insisted I kill my dog. I could only see it that way, that she was insisting I 'kill my dog'. And I had no choice—I had to take her on her final trip to the vet. Another bit of irony: later I read in the woman's memoirs of her anger and grief when her roommate, many years before, had demanded she *kill her dog*. She used those exact words. I wonder if she saw the irony?

As I write this and the memories have been laid bare before me, I find myself literally wringing my hands. (I didn't know people actually did that!) While the conscious memory of these things fades, I suspect the body has a clear memory of 'em all. And so with the pile up of three years of psychological pain, my body decided to grow some tumors. GDFSE.

"When your life falls apart, you can either grow or you can grow a tumor. I decided that instead of allowing my body to continue to manifest my stressors physically, it was time to finally wake up and do whatever it would take to finally get healthy, inside and out."
Lissa Rankin

You see, it has been important to me not to complain because I have had so many blessings in my life. Yes, I really have, and I have actually made a lifetime list with "Blessings" at the top of the page, and I add to it daily. Really I think perhaps I am terrified to complain for fear the gods will become angry and give me even more of what I don't want. And what I fear more than cancer is even less human contact. (I already have close to zero dog contact.) And I have not yet figured out the degree to which I can healthily 'feel the pain', without wallowing of course. As I write this, I am again feeling the pain.

After my second cancer arrived, I made my own personal "profit and loss" statement I guess you could call it, and put plenty of things in both columns.

Whitman wonders why, with all of the GDFSE part of my life, I didn't take up boozing, or a drug habit, or acted out with gambling, sex, or perhaps a life of crime. All the cliché stuff. I guess my drug of choice was soda with a side of fast food, both of which I still struggle with. Or perhaps Whitman will make me say "with both of which I still struggle? No. Uh... let's see... uh...

"Rock bottom became the foundation on which I built my life."
J.K. Rowling

Okay, well we all have our stories, but no point telling them and retelling them to ourselves every night as our own personal beddy-bye tales. No my-woe-is worse-than-your-woe because there are plenty of people out there who could win at that game. I have tried to keep a tight grip on my tales of woe to keep me going. But here I have gone on for four pages of woe, so what is my point?

1. I just feel like screaming it out. Finally.

2. It underscores my point about the relationship between cancer and trauma.

3. If you are going through trauma right now, and/or a diagnosis of cancer, the sun will come out again, says Pollyanna! (As a bit of a cosmic joke, outside it is pouring as I write this.) But we do need this cycle of rain and it smells and sounds wonderful (and even looks lovely from my 9th floor window.)

So hang in there, say both Pollyanna and Morticia. 'You can bet your bottom dollar...'

In Which I Mount My Soapbox
and Show My Cranky Side

"The necessity of teaching mankind not to take drugs and medicines is a duty incumbent upon all who know their uncertainty and injurious effects; and the time is not far distant when the drug system will be abandoned."
Charles Armbruster, M. D.

H G Wells created a world set in the distant future (the year 802,701 I believe) in his book *Time Machine* (I first came across the movie version decades ago) where civilization had split into two branches. There were gentle, submissive, humanoid creatures, not given to serious thought, called Eloi who lived above ground, and underground lived the fierce, warlike Morlocks. I remember there was a siren of some sort that called the Eloi underground where they were eaten or used in some other nefarious way by the Morlocks. (It has been many many decades since I saw the movie!) But I do remember a siren and the Eloi marching unquestioning to their fate.

The story of the Eloi and the Morlocks is such a perfect metaphor for those who go unquestioning to chemo and radiation as Big Pharma their money, gobbles them up and spits out their bones. And society does not question their path.

I invite all of you who are reading this book and just beginning your cancer journey *not* to let fear propel you into hasty decisions. This, I dare say, will be the most important decision of your life. In Susun S. Weed's excellent *Breast Cancer? Breast Health!* she says the first step when you get a cancer diagnosis: *Do nothing.* I'd add before you do *anything*, to just breathe it in, feel your power, feel your strength, feel the ultimate wisdom of your body. Give yourself a bit of time to get your sea legs. Weed continues: *"I asked myself is there any healing rule that everyone all over the world would agree to, and I couldn't come up with anything better than* first do no harm. *That seems to be a healing rule that we could all agree with. And so then I simply took every approach, every technique, every substance and I said, 'How much harm does it do?'"*

Perhaps the quickest way to become informed about the potential dangers of conventional cancer treatment versus all the other treatments that *honor* the body, is to watch the series *The Truth About Cancer* (thetruthaboutcancer.com). [Any doctors reading this book—you too, please.] Bombarding the body with chemo and radiation—especially "aggressive" cancer treatment, is like finding your beloved baby crying, then pinching it and slapping it to get it to stop crying. Your body is your beloved baby. If you have developed cancer, it is crying out to be loved and nourished, not tormented.

I have quite a bit of anger stored up against The Great Pharma Machine, and against the advertising showing smiling bald women in turbans as if what they were doing made sense, even as if they were having a good time. I deplore the pink kitsch that lures you to donate to research designed simply to feed the Morlocks. [Read about pinkwashing in the Pink Stinks chapter...]

FOLLOWING THE BRULES OF CANCER
"Language defines how we view the world. When you learn to hack language, you learn how to hack the world and your capabilities in the world. So one of the words I coined is a brule *which is a*

bullshit rule. A brule is a bullshit rule that we adopt to simplify our understanding of the world so we can play it safe so we don't have to create or non-conform. We can just blindly follow the path that everyone else has been following for generation to generation and be normal. The book* is about breaking the rules—it's about questioning what your teachers, your parents, your fathers, your preachers tell you to do. It is about setting your own rules for yourself and discarding the bullshit rules of the past."
from Vishen Lakhiani's **The Code of the Extraordinary Mind: 10 Unconventional Laws to Redefine Your Life and Succeed On Your Own Terms*

And this book too is about breaking the rules and questioning what we have been told, for we have been handed far too many brules in our cancer journey. It is time to question, time to create, time to step out of formation and dance to our own music!

I have always tended to be a rule breaker, to dance to my own music in my you're-not-the-boss-of-me fashion. When the Beatles first came to America, I was in ninth grade and I found all the screaming mobs quite tedious and I was determined not to go along with the crowds, not to become a Beatles fan. I successfully resisted for a couple of years, determined not to be swayed by mob rule. Eventually I became as big a fan as anyone, but on my own terms, in my own time. In the same way, I have never understood the lure of the 'trendy'. I mean, what is the attraction of fashion, anyway? Why would you want to look like everyone else? I do think this attitude has ended up potentially saving my life as I have adamantly resisted joining the Eloi as they marched relentlessly into the clutches of the Morlocks.

In my opinion, and in the opinion of many I respect, chemo and radiation do nothing to make you healthier or stronger or more whole. If you want 'Chemo Brain', Peripheral Neuropathy, Xerostomia, Dehydration, Anemia, Neutropenia, Thrombocytopenia, Alopecia, Lymphedema, Cardiomyopathy,

Skin Sensitivity, Infertility, a shredded immune system (just when you really need it!), Osteoporosis (shall I keep going?)—go get you some chemo. Take your pick—there is a lovely menu for you. You thought losing your hair and throwing up were the only price you had to pay to get well? Please, please do your own research on the potential for long-term damage from chemo and radiation. Lifelong damage. LIFELONG DAMAGE. Devastating problems can appear 5, 10 years after your last visit to the infusion room that were a result of chemotherapy, cancers that are the direct *results* of your treatment for cancer. Think about it: how could filling your body with poison NOT result in cancer? How many people do you know who died with cancer? Of those people, how many used conventional treatment? Still think it is a good idea? From what I have seen, a few people live IN SPITE of chemo, not because of it.

"It's the closest to death I have ever been. The chemotherapy takes you as far down to hell as you have ever, ever been,"
Melissa Ethridge

A groundbreaking 14-year study was published in the *Journal of Clinical Oncology* in December 2004 called "The Contribution of Cytotoxic Chemotherapy to 5-year Survival in Adult Malignancies. Results: The overall contribution of curative and adjuvant cytotoxic chemotherapy to 5-year survival in adults was estimated to be 2.3% in Australia and 2.1% in the USA." Are you prepared for potentially devastating side effects for those odds?

I have made a number of significant choices in the years following my ovarian cancer diagnosis in 2013 and kidney cancer in 2015. My first and most powerful choice was not to be a *victim* of cancer, not to see cancer as the enemy. My second choice and by far the easiest was not to do chemotherapy—under any circumstances.

On occasion someone will remark that that must have been a hard decision, that it was "brave", but really it was so easy that it was not even really a decision, which implies choosing between two or more viable options. Chemotherapy was never for one minute in the running. Almost every time I tell someone of my cancer diagnosis and my no-chemo decision, they breathe a sigh of relief—even, and maybe especially—the (non-MD) medical people—the nurses and other medical people with closer patient contact. It was as if they'd been holding their breath, respectfully refraining from comment until they knew my approach to the cancer. I live in Asheville, North Carolina, after all—a veritable hotbed of all things alternative, holistic, free-range, and *non-toxic*.

I will say that the doctors don't uniformly breathe a sigh of relief as they have been so well-indoctrinated. Vocabulary.com says *"Indoctrination means teaching someone to accept a set of beliefs without questioning them."* Interesting that both the word "indoctrinate" and "doctor" come from the Latin "docere"—to teach. In the process of creating new doctors, medical schools *indoctrinate* their doctors, no? Upon graduation, they receive their white coats, their stethoscopes, *and a set of blinders.* (Luckily, a growing number are rejecting the blinders.)

Medical schools and Big Pharma and society as a whole have seemed to collude to indoctrinate us, to dis-empower us. Doctors are forbidden to even hint that the "standard of care" might be less than ideal. I do believe that Big Pharma has them by the short hairs. Some doctors on the forefront of natural healing have actually been *killed,* so the others are forced to be especially careful in how public they are with their philosophy. Email me for a link to the living book for supporting documentation. I feel especially protective of my doctor who, I believe, turned down his or her set of blinders at graduation.

The tools of Big Pharma are all about harm. In the words of Susun Weed (author of *Healing Wise*), naturopaths everywhere, and most especially in the Hippocratic Oath—*Primum non nocere* (first, do no harm). Please consider making *Primum non nocere* your mantra. People are dying not just from cancer, but from the treatment for cancer! Losing your hair and throwing up are nothing compared with a lifetime of lymphedema, peripheral neuropathy, destruction of your immune system, permanent damage to organs like your heart and your liver. Let me count the ways, the potential side effects of chemotherapy: Congestive heart failure (CHF), Coronary artery disease, Arrhythmia—irregular heartbeat. *What are you thinking*, Western medicine? And think about it: what is considered "success" in cancer treatment in the allopathic world? Survival. I think they set the bar way too low at mere survival. Sometimes survival means "not quite dead" or even so sick you wish you were. How can doctors so completely abandon the Hippocratic Oath?

Here are a few subject titles from an online support group for women suffering through chemo for ovarian cancer:

I still have cancer :(/ Is treatment schedule ever shortened.. / Low blood platelets question / No news yet. / Neuropathy / Devastating News / Vanity Fair: A Matter of Life and Death by Marjorie Williams / Narrowing of colon at cecum?? Causes?? / Fridays corner - how do you know if you're a chronic cancer patient? / Could "storms" be porphyria? Answer?? Need help!! / After a cancer diagnosis, how to break the news – expert tips / Anaemia on carboplatin / Stage 2 Any Maintenance therapy after Frontline? / cm tumor found on PET/ct scan / How do you know it has reoccurred? / First Cancer Moonshot recommendation is more patient data / Blood pressure management during treatments / Doxorubicin allergy / Stable Malignant Moderate Plural Effusion / Unofficial poll re: survival after diagnosis / It's Not Good News / Other Disability Benefits? / How has your digestion of food changed? / Vision problems with chemo / Possible causes of the pelvic and back pain / How many Reoccurances / Stomach pain from Carboplatin / Looking to hear what day was worst for chemo effects / hospice

Do these women sound like they are on the road to healing? Or do we have a clear picture here of the Morlocks tormenting the Eloi?

AND ABOUT RADIATION...
Cancer.net says the "Doctors have safely and effectively used radiation to treat cancer for more than 100 years." and then proceeds to explain that the treatment could cause a new cancer later in life. Oh really? This is safe and effective?? They go on to say: "As internal radiation therapy causes the patient to give off radiation, a number of safety measures are necessary. Women who are pregnant and children younger than 18 should not visit the person receiving treatment. Other visitors should sit at least six feet from the patient's bed. They should also limit their stay to 30 minutes or less each day. Permanent implants remain radioactive after the patient leaves the hospital. Because of this, he or she should not have close or more than five minutes of contact with women who are pregnant and children for two months.

"The risk of radiation exposure to family and friends can be reduced by using the following precautions:
Washing hands thoroughly after using the toilet
Using separate utensils and towels
Drinking plenty of fluids to flush the remaining radioactive material from the body
Avoiding sexual contact
Minimizing contact with infants, children, and women who are pregnant"

This is insanity. This is NOT a cure for anything. This is welcoming in all kinds of damage to the body. Try googling COGNITIVE DISSONANCE and see how it applies here.

I don't understand why so many people are blind to the dangers of conventional treatment for cancer. There is something called Inattentional Blindness—perhaps you have heard of it? There is an article in Smithsonian Magazine September 2012 by Daniel Simons called *But Did You See the Gorilla? The Problem With Inattentional Blindness* which states that *the most effective cloaking device is*

The Vocabulary of Joy

the human mind. "Viewers of this video" Simon says, "were asked to count how many times white-shirted players passed the ball. Fifty percent of them didn't see the woman in the gorilla suit" [walking just as bold as you please right through the scene]. No photographic trickery, no smoke and mirrors. But 50% did not see what was right in front of them. So many don't seem to see the truth of chemotherapy and radiation, when it is as obvious as a woman in a gorilla suit—the 500 pound gorilla of Big Pharma you might say.

"Our hesitation to shift awareness is understandable. We've been in the Piscean age for the last 2000 years. We've received the constant instruction to not question authority and power. As we move into the Aquarian Age, we're shifting into an energy of connection, community, networking, and self-empowerment."
Jonna Rae Bartges

TIME FOR A SHIFT IN POWER
For too many years we have willingly surrendered our own power, our own authority, and lived as Eloi. We have been so totally divorced from our own intuition, our own guidance, always looking outside of ourselves to know what to do. That is slowly beginning to shift as evidenced by more and more people choosing to find their own way to healing. It is indeed "the dawning of the Age of Aquarius" I do believe. I used to sing that in my hippy days (or hippy wanna-be, hippy lite you might say).

So the epidemic of cancer has been a gift on a grand scale—even Big Cancer (the massive cancer industry) has been a gift—as their treatment of us has been so ill-advised, so egregious, so outrageous that we are pushed to finally say NO. NO MORE! and rediscover our roots, our deep connection with the Mother, with Grandfather Fire, and our own deep connection with all-that-is. In my life, those connections have been facilitated by my 44-year practice of Transcendental Meditation and studies with Maharishi Mahesh Yogi, by my more recent practice of qigong under the tutelage of Matt Kabat and Brian Lewis, and by my work with my Plant Spirit Medicine healer Lisa Lichtig. And those deep connections have been facilitated too by my built-in you're-not-the-boss-of-me attitude, which I believe has served me well.

Dr. Darrell Wolfe declared *"The American Medical Association has made Medical Doctors the equivalent of 'high priests', which leaves the majority of the population left to believe that only doctors hold the answers and the power to heal. The foundation on which medical health is now based, is absent of logic and is dis-empowering for those who do not question its self-ordained authority."*

TO RANT OR NOT TO RANT, THAT IS THE QUESTION
I have been warned by several people to go gently with my ranting against Big Pharma and the use of chemo and radiation. But I can't, I simply can't and be true to myself and to what I have learned is true. Again, please see the series *The Truth About Cancer* (thetruthaboutcancer.com)–probably the most complete and accurate indictment of Western medicine's deplorable treatments for cancer, and the healthy options that exist.

And speaking of 'treatment', it enrages me (and I don't 'enrage' as a rule) that it is assumed that the use of chemo and radiation is a foregone conclusion. Oh, you have cancer? Well then of course you are doing chemo and/or radiation. Right now I am looking for a bit of financial support from cancer non-profits, most of whom require that I am still 'in treatment'. What – your 'treatment' is found in the produce aisle? In fresh air and sunshine and birdsong? In love and laughter? What are you, some kind of a nut? I have had to explain again and again to such agencies that my 'treatment' of choice is to nurture my body, to regain balance and harmony, and I will continue this treatment for the rest of my life. And not in fear, but in joy. My goal is far greater than mere survival.

Last night I watched an outstanding presentation by a doctor who is a leader in Functional Medicine—and who years ago was my primary care doctor—Dr. Patrick Hanaway. He spoke eloquently of seeing the whole person in determining what was out of balance and looking first to nutrition to re-establish balance. My current doctor—Brian Ritchie Lewis—also a leader in integrative, holistic medicine, is also about seeing the whole person and looking to Big Pharma as a very, very last resort. I am heartened by this shift in medicine, though it is glacially slow and so long overdue.

Note this appalling deception from Big Cancer:

"Yet despite the mounting evidence of chemotherapy's lack of effectiveness in prolonging survival, oncologists continue to present chemotherapy as a rational and promising approach to cancer treatment. If receiving a treatment causes a patient's risk to drop from 4 percent to 2 percent, this can be expressed as a decrease in relative risk of 50 percent. On face value that sounds good. But another, equally valid way of expressing this is to say that it offers a 2 percent reduction in absolute risk, which is less likely to convince patients to take the treatment."
International Center for Nutritional Research, Inc.

My quarrel is not just with chemo and radiation; it is with a whole system that looks to the pharmacology lab rather than the abundance we find in nature for healing. I will now let some DOCTORS share their feelings about that topic.

"The cause of most disease is in the poisonous drugs physicians superstitiously give in order to effect a cure."
Charles E. Page, M.D.

"Medicines are of subordinate importance because of their very nature they can only work symptomatically."
Hans Kusche, M.D.

"If all the medicine in the world were thrown into the sea, it would be bad for the fish and good for humanity"
O.W. Holmes, (Prof. of Med. Harvard University)

"Every drug increases and complicates the patient's condition."
Robert Henderson, M.D.

"The greatest part of all chronic disease is created by the suppression of acute disease by drug poisoning."
Henry Lindlahr, M.D.

"Every educated physician knows that most diseases are not appreciably helped by medicine."
Richard C. Cabot, M.D. (Mass. Gen. Hospital)

"Medicine is only palliative, for back of disease lies the cause, and this cause no drug can reach."
Wier Mitchel, M.D.

"The person who takes medicine must recover twice, once from the disease and once from the medicine."
William Osler, M.D.

"Medical practice has neither philosophy nor common sense to recommend it. In sickness the body is already loaded with impurities. By taking drug - medicines more impurities are added, thereby the case is further embarrassed and harder to cure."
Elmer Lee, M.D., Past Vice President, Academy of Medicine.

"Our figures show approximately four and one half million hospital admissions annually due to the adverse reactions to drugs. Further, the average hospital patient has as much as thirty percent chance, depending how long he is in, of doubling his stay due to adverse drug reactions."
Milton Silverman, M.D.

The Vocabulary of Joy

In Which I Mount My Soapbox and Show My Cranky Side

(Professor of Pharmacology, University of California)
"Why would a patient swallow a poison because he is ill, or take that which would make a well man sick."
L.F. Kebler, M.D.

"Drug medications consist in employing, as remedies for disease, those things which produce disease in well persons. Its materia medica is simply a lot of drugs or chemicals or dye-stuffs in a word poisons. All are incompatible with vital matter; all produce disease when brought in contact in any manner with the living; all are poisons."
R.T. Trall, M.D., in a two and one half hour lecture to members of congress and the medical profession, delivered at the Smithsonian Institute in Washington D.C.

"It is simply no longer possible to believe much of the clinical research that is published, or to rely on the judgment of trusted physicians or authoritative medical guidelines. I take no pleasure in this conclusion, which I reached slowly and reluctantly over my two decades as an editor of The New England Journal of Medicine."
Harvard Medical School's Dr. Marcia Angell

and finally,

"What hope is there for medical science to ever become a true science when the entire structure of medical knowledge is built around the idea that there is an entity called disease which can be expelled when the right drug is found?"
John H. Tilden, M.D.

In Which I Declare That Pink Stinks

"What if everything we think we know about how the world works—our ideas of love, education, spirituality, work, happiness, and love—are based on Brules (bullsh*t rules) that get passed from generation to generation and are long past their expiration date?"
Vishen Lakhiani

I propose that most everything we know about cancer, or at least the knowledge that is in the public domain, has long passed its expiration date! A leader in the cancer propaganda machine is the Susan G. Komen Foundation. The Washington Post ran an article October 21st 2014 by Karuna Jaggar, executive director of Breast Cancer Action, a national organization advocating for women at risk of and living with breast cancer. The article was entitled *Komen is supposed to be curing breast cancer. So why is its pink ribbon on so many carcinogenic products?* In the article, Jaggar states:

> *"Pinkwashing has become a central component of the breast cancer industry: a web of relationships and financial arrangements between corporations that cause cancer, companies making billions off diagnosis and treatment, nonprofits seeking to support patients or even to cure cancer, and public relations agencies that divert attention from the root causes of disease."*

See resources online (in the living book) for a link to Barbara

The Vocabulary of Joy

In Which I Declare That Pink Stinks

Ehrenreich's rich and insightful *Welcome to Cancerland: A Mammogram Leads to a Cult of Pink Kitsch*. A sneek peek: *"Now breast cancer has blossomed from wallflower to the most popular girl at the corporate charity prom. Possibly the idea is that regression to a state of childlike dependency puts one in the best frame of mind with which to endure the prolonged and toxic treatments. Or it maybe that, in some versions of the prevailing gender ideology, femininity is by its nature incompatible with full adulthood-a state of arrested development. Certainly men diagnosed with prostate cancer do not receive gifts of Matchbox cars.*

"I can't seem to get enough of these tales, reading on with panicky fascination about everything that can go wrong-septicemia, ruptured implants, startling recurrences a few years after the completion of treatments, 'mets' (metastases) to vital organs, and-what scares me most is the short term-'chemo-brain,'or the cognitive deterioration that sometimes accompanies chemotherapy."

Big Pharma has its counterpart in the Susan G. Komen Foundation. When I am feeling especially cranky, I might even say that Monsanto has its counterpart in Komen.

From I Will Not Be Pinkwashed: Komen's Race Is for Money, Not the Cure [articles.mercola.com]:
> *"The multimillion-dollar company behind all those pink 'breast cancer awareness' ribbons -- the Susan G. Komen Foundation – uses less than a dime of each dollar to actually look for a breast cancer cure, as promised."*
>
> *"Plastering pink ribbons on every conceivable product has much more to do with raising awareness of, and money for, the Komen Foundation than it does curing breast cancer; pink ribbon campaigns are commonly used on products that may contribute to cancer, such as fried chicken and*

cosmetics that contain cancer-causing ingredients."

"There are no mentions of eating healthy foods, getting proper levels of cancer-preventing Vitamin D, or cutting out sugar — the substance that feeds cancer cells — in any of its "public health education" efforts. Even though these are scientifically proven ways to prevent cancer."

It's reported that the Komen Foundation owns stock in several pharmaceutical companies, including AstraZeneca, the maker of tamoxifen, a cancer drug that is actually classified as a human carcinogen by both the World Health Organization and the American Cancer Society. The more chemo you do, the richer Komen gets.

From thinkbeforeyoupink.org: *"Breast Cancer Action is the watchdog for the breast cancer movement. We are able to tell the truth about the epidemic because we are the only national breast cancer organization that does not accept funding from entities that profit from or contribute to cancer, including the pharmaceutical industry."*

The BCAM (Breast Cancer Awareness Month) idea 'was conceived and paid for by a British chemical company that both profits from this epidemic and may be contributing to its cause...'".

From Wikipedia: *"Sometimes referred to as National Breast Cancer Industry Month, critics of NBCAM (National Breast Cancer Awareness Month) point to a conflict of interest between corporations sponsoring breast cancer awareness while profiting from diagnosis and treatment. The breast cancer advocacy organization, Breast Cancer Action, has said repeatedly in newsletters and other information sources that October has become a public relations campaign that avoids discussion of the causes and prevention of breast cancer and instead focuses on 'awareness' as a way to encourage women to get their* mammograms. *The term pinkwashing has been used by Breast Cancer Action to describe the actions of companies which manufacture and use chemicals which show a link with breast cancer and at the same time publicly support charities focused on curing the disease. Other criticisms center on the marketing of 'pink products' and tie-ins, citing that more money is spent marketing these campaigns than is donated to the cause."*

In the New York Times, *"A Growing Disenchantment With October 'Pinkification'"* by Gina Kolata, October 30, 2015:
"fine print disclaimers on pink products sold by Dick's Sporting Goods reveal that in some instances, no money at all is donated to breast cancer research. Other companies cap the amount they give to research during each October's 'pink' campaign, but do not tell consumers when that cap has been reached." and Kolata goes on to say: *"many women with breast cancer hate the spectacle. 'I call it the puke campaign,' said Marlene McCarthy, the director of the Rhode Island Breast Cancer Coalition, who has metastatic breast cancer."*

Breast cancer awareness, critics charge, has become a sort of feel-good catchall, associated with screening and early detection, and the ubiquitous pink a marketing opportunity for companies of all types.

Stephen Colbert nails it: *"Anybody who knows me knows I am a huge supporter of the Susan G. Komen for the Cure foundation, which raises millions of dollars a year in the fight against breast cancer . . . So I'm giving a big Tip of my Hat to the Komen foundation for spending almost a million dollars a year in donor funds to sue these other groups. If they don't own the phrase "for the Cure," then people might donate money thinking it's going to an organization dedicated to curing cancer, when instead it's wasted on organizations dedicated to curing cancer."*

Sometime in the year before my ovarian cancer diagnosis, a friend posted on Facebook a call to donate to cancer and I gave him, I am afraid, a rather snarky response. He is a lovely guy and very well-intentioned, but too often people hear the word CANCER and reflexively open their pocketbooks. Cancer, like most things in life, is very complex. Research to find a cure is very complex. The "military-industrial complex" that is "Big Cancer" is, well, very complex. Throwing money their way without really knowing where is it going is like pissing in the wind. The book *The Emperor of All Maladies: a Biography of Cancer* by Siddhartha Mukherjee is a harrowing account, in my opinion, of the misunderstandings and missteps in the allopathic world's "war on cancer". Here in the 21st century we do indeed have a drug problem—with Big Pharma.

Okay, I am out of steam. I am going to leave this topic behind, for now. In the living book, I will continue to give information about how pink, for the most part, stinks.

In Which Psyche Meets Soma

"The 'holistic' aspect is what modern science is starting to refer to as systems biology, realizing that everything is interconnected, everything is a living system. Most ancient healing traditions such as Ayurveda, Native American, African, Tibetan, or Chinese medicine, have this worldview of interconnected living systems. Even the roots of Western Medicine in ancient Greece began with this premise."
Brian Ritchie Lewis, MD

"Healing is wholeness. To become more whole means it is not just whole within my body but whole within my relationship to all that is on this earth and in this universe."
Patrick Hanaway, MD

One of the greatest gifts of cancer for me has been that the fact that everything is interconnected has moved from a concept in my head and has taken up residence in my bones. I suspect that both Patrick Hanaway and Brian Lewis know it in their bones too. The concept was not new to me, but what I learned from these two men, and from my reading about the link between cancer and the psyche, from Joe Dispenza's *You Are The Placebo*, from Lissa Rankin's *Mind Over Medicine*, and from Turner's *Radical Remission*, has been icing on the cake.

But it was working with Lisa Lichtig, my Plant Spirit Medicine healer, and by extension her teacher, Eliot Cowan, that has had the most profound impact on my head-to-bones shift. Working with her is when I really began to open up to the deepest connections to the natural world, and it has been the most powerful mind/body/spirit healing in my cancer journey—my very best "chemo". Lisa is an MD, but in working with her she wears her Plant Spirit Medicine hat, not her stethoscope, and she has guided me from psyche to soma and back again, carefully interlacing the two. Her words have not appeared in these pages like those of Patrick Hanaway and Brian Lewis, but it is to Lisa first and foremost that this book is dedicated. My interactions with her have been way beyond words.

One of the (many) bones I have to pick with Western medicine's "standard of care" cancer treatment—it addresses only the physical aspect of cancer when cancer is clearly not just about the body. And while we are at it, if they claim their treatment is the thing to do, why are they still "waging war" on cancer? Everyone is making a big fuss about "the cure for cancer" but I suspect that if all of Big Pharma's labs worked around the clock for several centuries they'd not find "the cure"—because they don't understand the problem. Modern medicine is finally learning more about psyche (i.e., mind, emotions, and spirituality) and how it dances with soma (the body) even though this knowledge is actually many centuries old. 'Everything old is new again', I guess.

Patrick Hanaway tells us, *"The current medical framework talks about evidence-based medicine as though evidence only includes a randomized control trial, a construct that was developed in 1963 to help isolate all other variables and say what's the effect of this drug versus not this drug. So we need to look at evidence from a broader perspective, from a systems perspective."*

> *"Everything is alive and in relationship."*
> Scott Sheerin [healingmusicnow.com]

The Vocabulary of Joy

Like I said, I am getting love notes from the Universe. A thought just popped into my head to google "evidence based medicine" and "hogwash". I did, and I got 53,000 hits!

"President Obama has made it clear that his administration wants to raise fees for primary care physicians who spend time talking to patients, listening to them, and managing chronic illnesses." Maggie Mahar *Some Raise Concerns About Evidence-Based Medicine*

I am blessed with a primary care doctor—Brian Ritchie Lewis—who does not view me as a pile of organs with a head on top. Yet only 25% of his graduating class in medical school chose to adopt an integrative, holistic approach, and it was the same percentage in the graduating class of Dr. Chad Krisel, his partner in the practice. It astounds me that a physician, having been exposed this approach to medicine, would take any other approach. Dr. Lewis spends the talking/listening time that makes the best kind of doctor.

In the *Indian Journal of Psychiatry, Rahul Kumar and Vikram K. Yeragani write in Psyche and soma: New insights into the connection:*

"Integral physiology has to do with the synthesis of conventional physiology and how our individual psyches (i.e., mind, emotions, and spirituality) interact with the world around us, to induce positive or detrimental changes in our bodies. In a broader sense, the concept applies to the health of society as a whole. In the past two decades, biomedical research has changed our understanding of body systems. It has now come to light that there is a complex network of feedback, mediation, and modulation among the central and autonomic nervous systems, the endocrine system, the immune system, and the stress system. These systems, which were previously considered pristinely independent, in fact, interact at myriad levels. Psychoneuroimmunology (PNI) is an emerging

discipline that focuses on various interactions among these body systems and provides the underpinnings of a scientific explanation for what is commonly referred to as the mind-body connection."

The Cartesian model of 'body as machine' has done us a huge disservice. In fact, contemporary Western medicine's reductionist view of almost everything does us a disservice, most especially in the treatment of cancer. For example, when they find a plant that is useful in healing, their goal is to find the 'active ingredient'—totally unaware of the power of the whole. [Another rant, but I will cut it off here.]

You will find the *psyche meets soma* theme throughout the book. The concept is nothing new for the denizens of Asheville or to a huge and growing number of people. Somehow it seems to have missed much of the medical establishment...

THE ROLE OF STRESS
"If you are being chased by a rhinoceros, maximum stress is good. But if you spend life thinking there is a rhinoceros chasing you, then you are in trouble,"
Matthieu Ricard

"Depression is a partial surrender to death, and it seem that cancer is despair experienced at the cellular level."
Arnold Hutschnecker in *The Will to Live*

In my own life, because I have been meditating for more than four decades, I deal with very few rhinoceroses. They don't tend to chase me. But I have had large doses of despair from time to time. Well, two times really. My depression was situational. The you-know-what hit the fan twice in my life and it was that that brought me to my knees. I can easily imagine my cells just giving up the ghost, I was so broken. My gut tells me that cancer appears when there is a perfect storm, when A, B, C, and D all crop up in your life and collude to bring you down. Shakepeare tells us "there is nothing either good or bad, but thinking makes it so" and BC (before cancer) my thinking made a bad situation worse. But with the advent of cancer, I have learned to flip the switch; I have learned I can use my thinking to my advantage. This has been one of the gifts of cancer. And this is why I despair every time people go on at great length about the horrors of cancer. I am not being naïve — I know that the journeys with some cancers can be horrific, especially if a person is enduring the machinations of Western medicine. My point is that cancer does not *de facto* equal horror. Body and mind can work together to great advantage.

"There are more things in heaven and earth, Horatio, Than are dreamt of in your philosophy."
Hamlet Act 1, scene 5, William Shakespeare

In Which I Deal With My Doctors

"If there is a connection and development of a trusting relationship—someone that they can count on—to just walk with them hand in hand on that healing journey, then the opportunity for healing is already happening."
Patrick Hanaway, MD

I believe I have found the right balance of respect and independence in dealing with my doctors. My gynecologic oncology surgeon is warm, personable, and I suspect did an excellent job slicing me open and sewing me up. I had not one whit of pain following surgery—perhaps she gets the credit, perhaps the anesthesiologist. My only disappointment (and this is a big one) was that I was given no support with nutrition, even after asking specifically for guidance. But I had no hesitation telling her that I absolutely refuse chemo under any circumstances. She was respectful of my choice (or perhaps merely conciliatory).

A bit of irony... until the arrival of ovarian cancer, I had successfully avoided PAP smears to check for cervical cancer. (My cervix was fine.) I think I've had maybe two PAP smears in my life. When I was at Gallaudet University for my M.S., a pelvic exam was a requirement. I felt that my hooha was none of their business, and I successfully procrastinated all the way through getting my degree.

In Which I Deal With My Doctors

Now that I have ovarian cancer under my belt (uh, pun intended), for the last three years I have had to have a pelvic exam every three months. Dang. Perhaps this is some kind of divine retribution? At least they don't do that awful scraping. She just sticks her finger up there and feels around for any signs of cancer—it takes just a couple of seconds. Now at last it is only every SIX months, as my ovarian cancer is in remission. Sometimes I wonder why I have passively gone along with that. I think the next one I will stretch out to seven months, or even eight. So there.

Anyway, back to oncology docs. I've heard horror stories of doctors saying "You are crazy to turn this (chemo) down. I will not work with you," and the like. I have heard stories of doctors delivering devastating news deadpan from the doorway, and then scuttling away as quickly as possible, eyes downcast. Some doctors threaten death if you do not buy into chemotherapy. I did not have that experience at all, and for that I am grateful. In fact, one of the warmest, kindest doctors I have run into in my cancer journey (and the first to whom I said 'No chemo, no way!') was Dr. Jon Larrabee who was a resident when I was in the emergency room at the time of my diagnosis. He was so grounded, so gentle and warm and happy. (That's what I love in a doctor!) His smile said to me, "You are okay. We can deal with this." It was he who handed me the card of the woman who was ultimately my gyn/onc surgeon. Even better, he (along with a team of residents) saw me daily in the hospital. On my last day, he sat on my bed and just beamed healing at me, then gave me a big hug—so I literally experienced his bedside manner. (He is now fully-fledged, working at a local ob/gyn practice.) I had to laugh: the perfectly nice female resident you could tell felt obligated to give me a hug after Dr. Larrabee did. It was not grudging, but did not bubble up from within. That was okay though... it was sweet of her to go through the motions anyway.

THE OTHERS
When my kidney acted up, I added a urologist and a nephrologist

to the list. They were pleasant—no complaints. I especially enjoyed the nephrologist who wore a playful yellow polka dot bow tie.

I was most disappointed in my last appointment with my neurologist (so many *ologists*!). He is a delightful guy. A good friend had recommended him and told me how much she likes him. She calls him Dr. Honeypot—to his face! So when he walked in the door in my first appointment, I stuck out my hand and said "Dr. Honeypot, I presume?" He broke out in a huge grin and we had a great connection from then on. I saw him for two appointments and all was splendid—a great connection forming. Then on my six-month follow up, when I arrived I saw only his PA and I was p-issed. She was quite nice, but I had been really looking forward to reconnecting with 'Dr. Honeypot' on my continuing what-is-Julie's-brain-doing-now journey. Before my next six-month appointment, I will be sure I am seeing HIM, or I will cancel. [UPDATE: I did not get a guarantee of seeing him, so I canceled.]

One thing I eventually learned in the hospital is that I can choose and I can refuse. You'd think this would not have been such a surprise to an independent-minded person like me, but it was, especially since my personality includes a wide streak of you're-not-the-boss-of-me. In high school, because I preferred coffee with lots of cream and sugar, I decided I would simply not drink coffee, but maybe once or twice a year on special occasions. I will not allow myself to be led around by the nose by that addiction. Not even coffee is the boss of me. Recently I chose not to be afraid of needles and I now watch when they draw my blood. Fear of needles will not be the boss of me. I am at choice all the time—but sometimes I have to remind myself.

So I do not blindly follow my doctors' bidding. They are not, I have long since realized, omniscient. And they are not the boss of me! I pick the best doctors I can, I listen carefully, and then make up my own mind. Medical science keeps changing and learning from its own mistakes, and this is good as we should all keep learning.

But in the meantime, Western medicine is a perfect example of the blind men and the elephant: they look so closely at tusk or tail they miss the entire elephant. [My primary care docs are very much the exception!] One day Western medicine will wake up and see the entire elephant, but until they do, the poor, malleable Eloi will continue to be subjected to chemo and radiation by oncologists who don't know tusk from tail, I fear.

PHYSICIANS for the SOUL

"The greatest mistake in the treatment of diseases is that there are physicians for the body and physicians for the soul, although the two cannot be separated."
Plato

"...physicians can become healers by no longer remaining mere technicians of the human body, but by becoming alchemists of the soul."
Deepak Chopra

Because I cannot rely on my oncologist for support with my mind/body/spirit approach to cancer, I am relying instead rather heavily on my mind/body/spirit primary care doctor in his role as 'alchemist of the soul'. I have been especially blessed with my doctors Brian Ritchie Lewis, my primary care doctor, and his partner Chad Scott Krisel (my, uh, secondary primary care doctor), two physicians/alchemists for the soul for sure. They view their patients not merely as a collection of living, breathing Lego™ blocks, but as multi-dimensional humans at the intersection of body, mind, and spirit. I could not have better doctors.

Let me tell you why I love these guys and their practice (Integrative Family Medicine of Asheville—IFMA) so much. First, they don't wear white coats. I can understand why doctors in hospitals wear them since many are strangers when they walk into your room and best to know you are dealing with a doctor and not a janitor, but when it is your own primary care physician, I don't need to see a white coat to know he has a medical degree. Street clothes enhance the equal footing and the partnership in healing they foster. When I accidentally called him "Brian" in an appointment one day early on, I discovered that was by no means forbidden. Now they are both "Brian" and "Chad" to me. [However, he is sometimes "Brian" in my head and sometimes "Dr. Lewis". I will do my best to confuse you by sometimes referring to him as one, and sometimes the other.]

Their staff are afforded the same privilege, though of course they refer to them as "Doctor" when speaking with patients. And speaking of their staff, I love those women! It is such a joy to sit in the waiting area—alas, all too briefly for my taste as I love watching them. They are intent on their work but they are always joyful. They tend to be either smiling or laughing as they work, and when the doctors pop into that area, they join in. I daydream about being on their side of the glass, working and smiling and laughing along with them. I remember one day a couple of years ago, they were all huddled together in the front area learning a new computer system. I'd finished my appointment and was walking from the bathroom, back on their side of the glass. Every single one of them turned to me and smiled as I passed and I felt a tsunami of loving kindness directed at me. Chad namastéd me and I felt a giant boost of oxytocin from them all. That is not hyperbole. I truly felt a wave of healing energy from them.

My initial appointment with Dr. Lewis was more than two hours long—he even served me tea! It was my good fortune to be his very first "non-friend and family" appointment so I got first-day, first-patient treatment. My first call to them had been several months before the office was even built. A dear friend had recommended him when I asked if she knew of any good 'holistic' doctors taking new patients, and as luck would have it, he was just finished with residency and starting his own practice along with Chad Krisel, a like-minded, like-hearted doctor looking to set up

The Vocabulary of Joy

his practice too. Brian's first 'prescription' was Tulsi (Holy Basil) tea. This, I could tell, was a doctor after my own heart. Asheville tends to be a magnet for physicians who are 'alchemists of the soul'.

I am reading in *The Web That Has No Weaver* by Ted Kaptchuk, O.M.D. about Chinese Medicine. Kaptchuk states:
"In a chronic condition or for a condition what will require a lengthy course of treatment, the physician needs to be deeply acquainted with the patient. Inquiry concerning life behaviors such as the balance of activity, rest, diet, and food habits is important. Even more critical, the physician needs to know what animates a person, "what make him or her tick," what are the sources of strength and weakness, and what give his or her life purpose and meaning. This deeper layer of a person, usually involving the Spirit, can sometime reveal the clearest delineation of a pattern. The physician may need to know about significant relationships, sources of pleasure and self-worth major disappointments, major successes, important learning experiences, and how a person managed earlier illness."

IFMA's intake form is 11 pages long, including questions like *What do you do to relax/relieve stress? What hobbies or interests do you have? Spiritual beliefs/religious affiliations, past, and present? What are your sources of Comfort, Nurturing, and Connection? If you could change one thing in your life, what would it be?*

I suspect Brian has a fairly good idea of what makes me tick. When I started with IFMA in 2012, I was going through a rather rough period in my life, certain I was suffering the 'slings and arrows of outrageous fortune'. Dr. Lewis and his staff were healing balm to my wounds—they put much more than a Band-Aid on my emotional booboos. I doubt they have any idea how much their kindness helped me begin to regroup and unfold. The folks at IFMA were instrumental in luring me out of my cave and back to the land of the living.

Early on, when they started their monthly wellness classes, I was too afraid to attend. Afraid of what exactly, I am not sure. With the loss of my Work, I was feeling so separate from the rest of the world, an alien being with little in common with other people. Sometimes sitting in the waiting room, watching them through the glass, I was mostly aware of the glass, the separation from joyful camaraderie. 'I am here, by myself, and all the joy is over there where I cannot reach.' The glass did begin to melt over time as my focus shifted from the flat, cold plane of the glass to the people behind.

I like Dr. Lewis' youth (though it is somewhat disconcerting that I am old enough to be his mother!) With his youth comes the advantage of going through medical school in a more enlightened era—an era that has begun to embrace things holistic and integrative. Medical schools now even know a bit about nutrition! Dr. L chose to learn even more. And I love his ponytail! (How 'Asheville' can you get?!)

Dr. Lewis served as a volunteer teacher for at-risk youth through Americorps. In medical school, he co-founded the Integrative Medicine student group at UNC which organized educational seminars, retreats, and weekly classes. He facilitated regional events for students interested in Integrative Medicine, holistic living, and restoring humanism to medicine, he received a grant for studying the healing methodologies from the Himalayas and Tibet and on and on and on. He's been authorized to teach yoga, meditation, and basic medical qigong. In other words, he's your typical 'new age sensitive doctor'.

Now I did not set out for this chapter to be a paean to my doctor, but my incredibly astute editor Whitman said "The doctor characters I can see now are very much part of the book, so the more details you can add that paint them as real people, the better." and my friend Debra Roberts, on reading an earlier version of this chapter, implored me to dig deeper. So...

The Vocabulary of Joy

In Which I Deal With My Doctors

FEET TO THE FIRE

I am having a bit of a challenge with (I am so embarrassed to say this) sodas. Very bad for anyone, but especially lethal for someone with cancer. Brian has tried both stick and carrot to separate me from my sodas. Even humor. I told him at one point I was craving orange soda, and he said something about my Sunkist. Startled, I asked him how he knew that was my brand, and he told me he moonlights as the food police.

It must be challenging to be a doctor and watch an otherwise intelligent patient continue to do something so stupid. I even have two nurse friends who are on my case about the sodas. However, as I write this, I am on day 14 soda free! LATER: I fell off the wagon and am attempting to climb back on. EVEN LATER: I fell off again. And so it goes...

A BIT OF HISTORY

One summer day in 2013, (August 26, to be precise) I told Brian my appetite was non-existent (one day all I had to "eat" was one cup of ginger tea) and I was feeling puffed up. His voice and body shifted, he rolled a bit closer to my chair, and he made the shocking statement, "We need to consider the possibility of cancer." Okay the truth is I don't remember his exact words, but that, I think, was the gist. I immediately back pedaled, saying that really, I just didn't have the energy to cook, and I was all right. He had the good grace to not actually roll his eyes, but I suspect he was doing a mental eye roll...

I wonder what it was like to introduce the topic of cancer to a patient. Did his heart speed up, did his jaw clench? And I wonder how he felt when I refused to address it. I don't know that I was afraid so much as that cancer seemed so, well, complicated. Cancer would probably send me down a rabbit hole of tests and delicate issues and I just was not ready to deal with it. I more or less dismissed the topic in my mind. Did he worry about his obligation as a physician and wonder how far he should push me?

He'd only been in his practice for a year and a half then. I wonder how many people he'd used the "C" word within that first 18 months. Did he watch me walk out the door and wonder what was to become of me, and how long I'd persist in denying the cancer? Exactly one month later, though, I called the office saying I still had no appetite and was even more bloated. They told me "Get in here *now*." Brian was fully booked that day so I saw Chad. He asked some questions, thumped my belly, and left the room lickety-split to order a CT scan. Brian, despite having back-to-back patients, poked his head in and had his turn at thumping me on the belly. I remember grinning, still not taking it seriously, telling him that Chad had gone off to order a CT scan, and he confirmed that was the thing to do. When I laughed, I wonder if he felt the urge to shake me and say "Get serious! It's cancer, stupid!"

Cancer is a delicate dance, both with the disease and with the doctor. Does the doctor ever just long to sit that one out?

> *"Each patient carries his own doctor inside him."*
> Norman Cousins, Anatomy of an Illness

In spite of Dr. Lewis' excellent mind/body/spirit skills, essentially I have been my own "doctor", researching and carrying out my own cancer "treatment". That has been empowering, reinforcing the idea that I am my own best healer. At the same time, part of me sometimes spins around, wide-eyed, looking for help, wanting a closer partnership in healing. Sometimes I think "Good grief, I have CANCER, and I am alone in dealing with this. This is not a cold. This is not the flu. This is C A N C E R." My oncologist doesn't deal with natural healing and Brian doesn't deal with cancer, so I have fallen through a big, giant crack. Essentially I am hung out to dry because the medical establishment refuses to allow doctors to wander off the trail. But that passes, and I realize (with a resigned whimper) that my glass is half full, and my health is ultimately best left in my own hands. I suppose.

In Which I Deal With My Doctors

Life is complex, the cancer journey is complex, and sometimes I hold somewhat contradictory opinions. "Help me!" "Go 'way and let me chart my own course." "PLEASE HELP ME!" Perhaps I am not the easiest of patients. (Can you say 'cognitive dissonance'?)

Okay, I see I have gotten distracted here—back to my relationship with my particular doctors. When I speak of doctors and elephants, I am NOT speaking of any doctor I have mentioned by name. They all see the WHOLE elephant and I am so blessed to be (or to have been) in their care. The signature on Dr. Lewis' email says: *'To heal our healthcare we will need to heal our culture. This process begins with the choices that we make in each moment. When we become aware of what drives our choices, and choose what supports health, we begin to nurture a culture of wisdom that is sustainable. This wisdom culture is a beautiful gift for all of our relations and descendants. Your everyday choices are your most powerful votes. Open to this possibility and remember the strength of your mundane actions. Live wisely for yourself and others.'*

With all the things going on with my body since 2010, my relationship with my doctors is of utmost importance to me. Because I am charting my own cancer course and because the AMA brings such pressure to bear on doctors to follow the "standard of care", I may be providing a significant challenge for Dr. Lewis—I may be a bit of an albatross around his neck. But he once said: "Each person is like a small community. We find the natural strengths, the perceived obstacles and the real obstacles, and work with them." I'd say the same: with my doctors I, too, find their natural strengths, perceived and real obstacles, and work with them.

> "People pay the doctor for his trouble;
> for his kindness they still remain in his debt."
> Seneca

In Which My Fork Leads the Way

"...we can change the way we make and get our food so that it becomes food again—something that feeds our bodies and our souls. Imagine it: Every meal would connect us to the joy of living and the wonder of nature. Every meal would be like saying grace."
Michael Pollan
The Omnivore's Dilemma: A Natural History of Four Meals

Tamoxifen vs turmeric; chemo vs carrots. Easy peasy – the choice is SO obvious! The very first step in my healing journey was to explore what I put on my plate. Michael Pollan sums it up in seven words: "Eat food. Not too much. Mostly plants."

I was fairly knowledgeable about diet BC (Before Cancer) but practice what I preach? Not so much. While I loved nutritious, fresh, whole foods, that was not always what filled my plate. In fact, twice in the last six years I lived on nothing but bologna sandwiches when that was all I could afford. Even now, at the end of the month I will sometimes be forced to chow down on high-fructose corn syrup laced food from the local food bank. (Their sign says something about offering "healthy foods", but again, not so much.)

In Which My Fork Leads the Way

My doctor and I both want me to be off of wheat, if not all grains, but there is often free bread in the community room in our basement (I live in subsidized senior housing) and I eat it when my cupboard is particularly bare.

It is an interesting dance with food I have now. I never thought I'd actually go hungry, and sometimes, *on rare occasions*, I do. And I have developed a shortage mentality *vis à vis* food. (Hey! How often do you get to casually throw around *vis à vis*?)

Now don't go thinking I am too pitiful: at the beginning of the month I have lovely fresh, organic, locally grown food thanks to some very dear friends in Florida who put money on my motherearthproduce.com account. And very dear friends right here in town share the beautiful organic produce from their garden when they can. It is feast or famine. I sometimes look at people's abundant food photos on Facebook and cry. Or salivate. (There is some water coming out of my face somewhere.)

Now (at the beginning of the month) when I shop for groceries I head straight to the produce section—the organic section of produce—armed with the Environmental Working Group's lists of *The Clean Fifteen and The Dirty Dozen*: those fruits and veggies that are fairly pesticide-free or have thick skins, as opposed to foods like apples that, if conventionally grown, are chock full of things you *do not* want inside your body. [See ewg.org for more information.]

I have given up processed foods (almost anything in boxes and cans) and now focus on food I could have plucked right from the soil. In fact, I learned to like kale when I lived with a friend who had a veggie garden in her front yard. When I walked out the front door and headed to the car, I'd stoop down, pinch off some fresh organic kale, and pop it in my mouth.

I focus on foods that are alkaline, green and leafy or colorful, and, if at all possible, local. And local of course dictates that it be seasonal. Turmeric is my go-to seasoning. It has been shown to be more powerful than chemo and for many, many things—not just cancer. NOTE: it is vital to include black pepper and a healthy fat (olive oil, coconut oil, etc.) with turmeric for it to be bioavailable.

I learned that many seeds we tossed or spit out in the past we should have been chewing and swallowing. In fact, seeds are often one of the richest parts of the plant. Chia seeds (remember chia pets?) and especially hemp seeds are good to incorporate in your three squares. So are flaxseeds, freshly ground and eaten within 15 minutes. Pumpkin seeds and sunflower seeds are yummy and nutritious. Everything raw, if you please. Processed food is a four-letter word. Many seeds as well as the skin or the area right beneath the skin that we have been peeling off for years are very good for us.

There is so much we have gotten wrong: margarine, for example. So many recipes (from the past especially) say 'butter or margarine'. I have never in my life bought margarine and I don't think my mother did either. Yuck. Check out the living book for a link to an excellent article by Andrew Weil on the subject.

All the way back in high school (my first stab at healthy eating) I went through our cabinets and tossed everything with MSG, so that has not been building up in my body either. ANOTHER NOTE: MSG hides in a number of different disguises. Sometimes it is called x and sometimes y.) Look up the hungryforchange.tv article SNEAKY NAMES FOR MSG (CHECK YOUR LABELS!).

Avocados and coconut oil were maligned for years, only now we know they are healthy and full of essential fats. Lowfat was the thing to do for decades, but now we know that when they reduce the fat, they add plenty of things we don't want. It is the type of fat that should concern us. [See Dr. Mark Hyman's books to learn more.] Nuts and seeds are nutrition powerhouses. Selenium is important for folks dancing with cancer and the RDA can be provided easily with 3 Brazil nuts a day.

Farewell my beloved grilled cheese sandwiches! Both grains and dairy are now on my very-rarely-if-at-all list.

I choose to follow Ayurvedic guidelines which discourage drinking with meals and drinking or eating cold things so I don't quench the digestive fire. (They are very big on digestive fire, the Ayurvedic folk.)

Not everything I eat necessarily directly "kills cancer", but my plan is to honor my body 'like I have never honored it before' and fill it with the freshest, most nourishing food so it can do its job and re-establish balance and harmony. Think anti-inflammatory, think 80% alkaline and read up on acid vs alkaline foods, think Mediterranean. Think colorful. Don't think bologna sandwiches.

Get a good water filter and keep it flowing. Berkee is one of the good ones. Water is a powerful healer. Look up the amazing work of Masuru Emoto!

The best single go-to book for eating for cancer is Kris Carr's *Crazy Sexy Diet. Don't rely on this chapter—it is just the tip of the iceburg.*

> *"If it came from a plant, eat it;*
> *if it was made in a plant, don't."*
> Michael Pollan

THE CHICKENS HAVE COME HOME TO ROOST
Dang those chickens. My primary care doctor, Dr. Lewis, says my triglycerides are elevated, likely due to sugar. I admitted that not only am I still drinking sodas but I have leapt back into soda drinking with wild abandon. As I write this I am now fourteen days soda free! Dang, I miss them. It is not easy. At least I don't have

any physical symptoms like a headache from caffeine withdrawal. My healing-cancer-naturally group I am sure would be horrified. We all know sugar is horrible for cancer. Well for just about anything, really. Obviously I don't always practice what I preach.

A WORD ABOUT MEAT

Speaking of plants, what about meat? At the moment, I am still eating meat but only pastured, free-range, treated-with-respect-and-kindness meat. And dairy. That may change. But since factory-farmed meats come from animals that are cruelly treated and full of hormones and other, uh, crap, I don't eat them anymore. I agree wholeheartedly with Wendell Berry who said

"I dislike the thought that some animal has been made miserable to feed me. If I am going to eat meat, I want it to be from an animal that has lived a pleasant, uncrowded life outdoors, on bountiful pasture, with good water nearby and trees for shade."
Wendell Berry, What Are People For?

and Michael Pollan who said

"... the way we eat represents our most profound engagement with the natural world. Daily, our eating turns nature into culture, transforming the body of the world into our bodies and minds."
Michael Pollan, The Omnivore's Dilemma:
A Natural History of Four Meals

A year or so ago I started a support group for people who want to heal their cancer naturally; there are now 189 of us and growing. I just moved us from a meetup group to Facebook (find us at facebook.com/groups/healingcancernaturally). At the moment we meet every second Saturday in my ballroom (called the roof garden on the beautiful 14 story, 94 year old building that is now my home.

We are a rather knowledgeable group and while we sometimes

have guest speakers come in, much of what we learn about food and other natural, cancer specific treatment, we learn from each other.

Dr. T. Colin Campbell, Professor Emeritus of Nutritional Biochemistry, Cornell University and author of *The China Study* (along with Thomas Campbell, MD)—says that our government should be discussing the idea that the toxicity of our diet is the single biggest cause of cancer. And yet all 'Big Cancer' organizations like Susan G. Komen focus on is early detection (that is, go-get-your-mammagram—which have been shown to be more risk than reward). So, mammagrams, then chemo and radiation, but nothing about prevention. P R E V E N T I O N, folks. Help us out, here. Give us some *useful* information. Don't just label us Eloi and send us through the Big Cancer money-making machine.

Breathe, Julie. Count to ten. Ahhhh.

GRATITUDE
If I had to choose a desert-island book, it would be *Earth Prayers From Around the World: 365 Prayers, Poems, and Invocations for Honoring the Earth* edited by Elizabeth Roberts and Elias Amidon. On page 2, they say:

> *"These prayers seek to heal the division that has grown between us and the rest of nature. They tell us: Pay attention. Attend to the relationships alive among all forms of life. Use imagination to explore the binding curve that joins us together. Seek to know the other. Join with it. Care for it as for yourself. When the human spirit is understood in this sense, as the mode of consciousness to the planet as a whole, if becomes clear that our entire life is an Earth Prayer."*

Prayer before a meal is my celebration of becoming part of the Earth and the Earth becoming part of me. It is a daily reminder that all is one, and that healing is about becoming one with nature.

What I put on my plate was the natural beginning of my healing journey and also symbolic of that union with all-that-is.

"The atmosphere, the earth, the water and the water cycle—those things are good gifts. The ecosystems, the ecosphere, those are good gifts. We have to regard them as gifts because we couldn't make them. We have to regard them as good gifts because we couldn't live without them."
Wendell Berry

In Which I Begin To Move

"We see in order to move;
we move in order to see."
William Gibson

There I was on the playground in first grade when my best friend, Sheba Leas, told me I ran funny. She was not being mean, she was simply observing, with a 6-year-old's matter-of-fact, frank appraisal, that I 'ran funny'.

And with my 6-year-old's naïveté, I believed her, and even now as a 66 year old, I suppose that belief has not entirely faded away. True or not (and I do have a vague memory of running wearing petticoats, and trying to hold my dress down as I ran to be 'ladylike') I allowed her pronouncement to color my entire life.

Consequently, I have almost always shied away from moving in public. I don't dance, even in a room by myself, as I have always believed I probably 'dance funny'. In high school when I swam, I'd swim underwater as I was less visible that way, because of course I must 'swim funny' too (even though I typically swim sans petticoats).

And we won't even talk about sex...

So here I am with two kinds of cancer under my belt, and I decided it was time to move beyond my 6-year-old persona and, well, *move*. I started with the LiveStrong at the Y program for people with cancer. Twelve of us dancing with cancer met twice a week for twelve weeks at my local Y. Me—at the Y! It took something like cancer to finally get me there. But at that point I was already needing to use a walker for balance, so now I actually walk funny.

Ironic, isn't it, that I am so firmly wed to the term "dancing" with cancer, yet in real life that is something I just can't do...

Anyway, I fell—splat—during the pre-test at LiveStrong. Stopped the whole test as folks came running over to see if I had injured anything more than my funny bone. Oddly enough, that fall helped me break through any lingering issues about movement, at least in that class. I stood up, dusted myself off, and laughed. I was using the walker with four wheels, (as opposed to my compact, travel walker with two wheels and two feet) and it got away from me in a tight turn as I had been feeling a bit competitive with my walkerless cancer compadres.

What I valued most about the folks in my Livestrong group was hanging out with a group of people with cancer—that was a first for me. I was still such a cancer newbie. They were men and women, a variety of ages, and everywhere from newly diagnosed to their cancer having been diagnosed a decade or more ago.

A TANGENT ABOUT BREASTS
Ultimately I had very little in common with the folks in my LiveStrong group as I was the only one out of a group of 12 going all natural, and the only one out of a group of 12 without a 'loved one' as caregiver, which pushed my self-pity button—bigtime. (Actually I have *no* potential caregivers.) I did feel a bit the odd woman out.

Near the end of the program, one woman in the group implored the rest of us to have our mammograms. I bit my tongue close to the point of blood running down my chin. I so wanted to shout that mammograms have been shown to be a Bad Idea, leading to false positives and unneccessary procedures and needless radiation which means mammograms can actually CAUSE cancer.

"As reported in a September, 2015 study in JAMA Internal Medicine article, researchers studied 16,120,349 women over the age of 40 who resided in 547 counties across the U.S. during a one-year period. The researchers correlated their findings with breast cancer incidence and mortality data during the ensuing 10 years. The scientists found a direct correlation between screening mammography and breast cancer incidence. In fact, they found a 16% mean increased incidence of breast cancer in women screened with mammography. However, there was no significant change in mortality in those screened with mammography. The authors noted, 'Although it has been hoped that screening would allow breast-conserving surgical procedures to replace more extensive mastectomies, we saw no evidence supporting this change.'" David Brownstein MD

From breastcancerfund.org/clear-science/radiation-chemicals-and-breast-cancer/ionizing-radiation.html: *"Evidence from studies of medical exposures to radiation as well as large-scale tragedies such as the atomic bomb in Japan have demonstrated that radiation can cause breast cancer."*

The danger of mammograms is at this point widely known, but alas, this is yet another example of the Morlocks and the Eloi. [See *In Which I Mount My Soapbox and Show My Cranky Side.*]

Yes, granted there is a variety of opinions on this topic... I have chosen to make my own decision based on those people I trust most and my own intuition and I have concluded that mammograms are a Very Bad Idea.

PARDON MY TANGENT

I was very touched when I learned that the LiveStrong program costs I believe $500 per participant, paid for by community donation. The program was well structured in that it included not only the machines in the Y but yoga-like exercises as well as exercises for the (emotional) heart—a workout for both pysche and soma.

Huff and puff machines are not my forte, however. I suppose they have their place, but what I am drawn to is something like qigong, with its gentle, peaceful nature. Its movement is counter-intuitive for many Westerners, but is actually more effective. In other words, running marathons and the like actually wastes chi.

CHI WHIZ

Qigong came along for me the following year. [NOTE: "Qi" is sometimes spelled "chi" and is pronounced chee.] Actually, my first exposure to qigong was back in 1999 when I took my mother to a weekend Medical Qigong class, shortly before we realized she was 'coming down with' ALS.

About that time a close friend taught me other aspects of qigong like the Inner Smile, the Microcosmic Orbit, and the healing sounds associated with each of the major organs. In recent years, I had started studying qigong again, this time excellent classes with Lara Diaz. Movement! Breath! Intention! No, not with an aerobics instructor's shouted "5 more! 4 more! 3 more!". It is really more like "movement..... breath..... intention..... ". Smooth and full of grace and very, very powerful.

Now qigong has come to me! I am studying with a wonderful qigong/tai chi teacher, Matt Kabat and... are you paying attention? My primary care doctor, Brian Lewis! Right here in my own building, in our rooftop ballroom every Thursday from 6:15 to 7:30. (What, YOU don't have a rooftop ballroom?! YOU don't have a very cool, very pony-tailed doctor who teaches qigong?)

From the national Qigong Association's website:

> *"Qigong is an ancient Chinese health care system that integrates physical postures, breathing techniques and focused intention.*
>
> *The word Qigong (Chi Kung) is made up of two Chinese words. Qi is pronounced chee and is usually translated to mean the life force or vital-energy that flows through all things in the universe.*
>
> *The second word, Gong, pronounced gung, means accomplishment, or skill that is cultivated through steady practice. Together, Qigong (Chi Kung) means cultivating energy, it is a system practiced for health maintenance, healing and increasing vitality."*

And they continue with: *"People do Qigong to maintain health, heal their bodies, calm their minds, and reconnect with their spirit."* The very essence of mind body spirit healing, qigong is also cancer-specific! Google cancer and qigong. Matt's qigong teacher YangYang is on staff at Memorial Sloan Kettering, perhaps the most respected cancer center in the country.

And I can do qigong in 'public'! Maybe I don't 'do qigong funny'! Or maybe I do, but people in my class are gracious enough not to point that out to me. Funny or not, I have come to know that qigong is essential for my healing. I do have to sit down most of the time because my balance (or lack thereof) makes me wobble so. I am still in qigong kindergarten, but the dance of movement and breath and intent is slowly becoming the basis of how I live my life.

"Too much action with too little intent makes for wasteful exertion of energy and the confusion between movement and progress."
Steve Maraboli, *Life, the Truth, and Being Free*

Julie Savage Parker

"Do less and accomplish more"
Maharishi Mahesh Yogi

WRITING AS HEALING
As I write this chapter, I have a memory of working with a
Transformational Kinesiologist at the turn of the century (I love
saying that!). When he asked me what about myself I wanted
to work on, after sifting through my perceived issues, I startled
myself when I came up with 'dance'. I wanted to dance! Or at least
move through space with a modicum of grace. Fear of dance,
I decided, was a major rock in my shoe as I walked my healing
journey.

AND IT WORKED! I stumbled on yet another form that
represented another form that deftly interwove *"inner, outer,
forward, back, physical, emotional, intellectual"* when I found
myself attending a Gabrielle Roth 5Rhythms dance class—I dove
straight into the deep end!! From 5rhythms.com:

*"5Rhythms is a dynamic movement practice—a practice of being
in your body—that ignites creativity, connection, and community.
While a seemingly simple process, the 5Rhythms practice facilitates
deep and unending explorations, moving the dancer beyond self-
imposed limitations and isolation into new depths of creativity and
connection. ... Waves move in patterns. Patterns move in rhythms.
A human being is just that—energy, waves, patterns, rhythms.
Nothing more. Nothing less. A dance.... The fastest way to still
the mind is to move the body... 5Rhythms transcends dance—
movement is the medicine, the meditation and the metaphor.
Together we peel back layers, lay our masks down, and dance till
we disappear. The 5Rhythms are a map to everywhere we want to
go—inner, outer, forward, back, physical, emotional, intellectual—
they reconnect us to the wisdom of our bodies and unleash
movement's dynamic healing power."* Gabrielle Roth

Just reading that I feel myself washed in waves of warm, liquid bliss. Lordy! Which reminds me, next week I am starting water physical therapy in a 94° pool. Umm... I foresee the bliss of the womb...

Oh my! Reading the website (because I am writing this chapter) has reawakened my longing to do that. Writing=Healing. Whole new chapters of Julie are being written. Amen and hallelujah!

In Which I Get By With a Little Help From My Friends

"Illness is the proving ground of friendship."
Letty Cottin Pogrebin

I t occurred to me that dancing with cancer is a bit like running a marathon. The job of running the race is mine, but the roads are lined with people, arms outstretched, offering me water for the journey.

Here are some highlights (*but by no means limits*) of some of the different ways my friends have 'offered me water'.

- My friend TB picked me up in the early morning to take me to my nephrectomy surgery, laughing with me as they wheeled me into OR and then staying with me all night, getting what sleep she could in the stiff recliner in my hospital room.

- My friend JN took me to my first surgery and picked me up, and is perhaps the most present in daily 'watching over me'. And she was the one who threw me a funeral! (Okay, okay... 'celebration of life'.)

The Vocabulary of Joy

In Which I Get By With a Little Help From My Friends

- My friend PF is always there for me when I need help... she even (blush) adjusted my diaper as it threatened to fall off when she picked me up from another hospital stay. They had given me medication that threatened diarrhea. I never had an accident, but she was picking me up in a Very Nice Car, so I chose to 'diaper up' on leaving the hospital... just in case.

- DR always holds a very powerful, unwavering vision of my wellness and my Sacred Next and shares it with me. She is my most persistent cheerleader!

- LL sent some magnificent flowers for my last surgery... they lasted a very long time and brought me much joy.

- DD made me apple sauce and soup to keep me nourished after my first surgery and drove me to the emergency right before my first diagnosis and stayed with me until 3 in the morning. She took me to my first CT scan and "held my hand". And she drove me to Duke to see the neurologist. *A whole day*, all the way to DUKE.

- DT was so present (even though she lives many miles away), so generous, and even found a way to get an email message to me in the hospital!

- LM told me about the beautiful place I am living now—at last, a place to be still and find my center.

And so on... Each friend has different strengths and together I have a terrific support system.

I have heard complaints from people with cancer about how sometimes people abandon them when they are diagnosed with cancer, or say inappropriate or thoughtless things. I have had nothing but kindness in words and deeds from people. I remember years ago when a friend told me she had bladder cancer. I wonder if my response was what she wanted/expected? (She went the conventional slash/burn/poison route, suffered terribly, and died. One friend with cancer who went slash/burn/ poison lived but the rest suffered and died.)

I hesitate to note, but from the friends (and cousins, my only family) *with whom I am not in regular contact*, I have not heard a peep. I know that they know. But really, I can understand their position. If I heard that one of them was diagnosed with cancer, I am not sure that I would get in touch, or what I would say, at least before I had been dipped in cancer myself. At this point in my 'cancer career', the last thing I would want to hear is the sort of "Oh no, oh no, how horrible, I am praying for you!" — the kind of thing that focuses on fear and victimhood. And they have their own lives, their own issues. Now that I think about it, I want to spend some time thinking what I might say to a friend newly diagnosed with cancer. Cancer is so prevalent here in the 21st century, I am likely to face that possibility.

One thing cancer taught me was that I have chosen my close friends wisely. Each one is a different piece of the puzzle of my life and each has different gifts to offer. No one abandoned me because they could not handle having a friend with ovarian cancer — 'the silent killer' (cue the melodramatic music!). My friends have been so kind and so helpful that it did flash through my mind to ask myself if I had manifested this cancer just so people would come running.

When it came time to 'announce' I had cancer, I paused for a moment, thinking I wanted to tell only those who would have just the right attitude: positive, supportive, the okay-this-is-a-bump-in-the-road, but-what-is-next crowd. This, being Asheville, is what I got. No one screwed up her face and gave me the hangdog eyes while planning what to wear to my funeral. (Okay, JN actually threw me a funeral and that was wonderful – more on that in *In Which I Attend My Own Funeral.*)

In Which I Get By With a Little Help From My Friends

I wonder what role expectation plays... Is it what-you-expect-is-what-you-get? I expected positive support from my friends, and that is what I got. I expected smooth, pain-free surgery, and that is what I got. I expected to enjoy my stay in the hospital, and that, too, is what I got. And most of all, I expected to heal... and that is what I got.

In Which I Attend My Own Funeral

Shortly after my first cancer surgery, my friend Julia Nooe felt I should have a "Celebration of Life"—and that I should be invited to the party. No one thought I was on my way out, but cancer being rather a big deal, I guess we all thought a bit more seriously about death. And my prognosis was a mystery at that point and I suppose still is, but the news is consistently good with each checkup. But shortly after my surgery, I had begun thinking about what friend was going to inherit which nick-nack. Since I have no heirs, I very much liked the idea that my friends would enjoy a little something that had brought me pleasure after my body was gone. No, I was not assuming that death was around the corner, but I was looking to my future (or lack thereof) to leave some kind of legacy, even if it was just a vase or a painting. Having no children, I guess it was my feeble attempt at 'immortality', or at least I'd be hanging around a bit in physical form, even if only by proxy, via my 'stuff'. My friends all refused to 'put their name' on anything—frustrating at first, but ultimately comforting. My doctor refused to discuss the disposition of my body. I had it in mind to donate myself to his medical school, but he would not discuss it— again frustrating at first, but ultimately comforting.

Julia, in the meantime, was insistent that we throw a party. "Celebration of Life" is, of course, a more uplifting title, but I

The Vocabulary of Joy

persisted in yanking her chain by calling it my funeral. I mean really, how many of us get to attend our own funeral?

I wanted to keep the number somewhat small so I would actually have time to connect with each person, so I limited the guest list to 12 people, more or less. I invited all my closest (local) friends and my beloved cousin Katherine and her husband Jim came all the way from DC for the occasion. Katherine's mother and mine were sisters, and as both of us are sisterless, we sort of serve as foster-sibs for each other. This gathering of dear friends felt like a gathering of beloved family, something, having no family of my own, I never get to experience. And because I had been alone every year this century (with very few exceptions) at the typical family gathering times— both Thanksgiving and Christmas—I requested a traditional turkey dinner. I loved the gathering of friends and I loved my friends meeting each other. The day was a powerful coming together of people who'd just as soon I stick around a while. Being so soon after diagnosis and major surgery, it was a somewhat strange time in my life—I felt I was on the cusp of something. The rules of engagement of my life were shifting, and I was busy finding my footing.

The funeral/celebration was held in the warm, inviting living room of the house were I was living with Julia serving as mistress of ceremonies. My dog Anna was in heaven with all the knees to sniff. And I got to hear all my eulogies! A few poor souls did not get the word that a eulogy was going to be expected, but they extemporized beautifully. Cole (16), the handsome son of my housemate Diane Douglas, sang and played the guitar for me, my favorite piece: Leonard Cohen's *Hallelujah*. His sweet sister Emily (6) played the piano for me and then played a duet with her mom.

We had a good time and I really feel no need for an actual funeral —the one I will be unable to attend (due to a previous engagement). I strongly recommend having your funeral *before* you die!

In Which I Learn About Post-traumatic Growth

"Sometimes out of catastrophe comes creativity."
Brian Ritchie Lewis, MD

*"Healing Crisis as Transformation… utilized intentionally
as the tipping off point, it can be like a graceful catapult
into the next gorgeous chapter."*
Karen Savage Shane

*"Something very beautiful happens to people when their world
has fallen apart: A nobility. A humility. A higher intelligence
emerges at just the point where our knees hit the floor."*
Marianne Williamson

In speeches in 1959 and 1960, John F. Kennedy popularized the meme about the word "crisis" in the Chinese language, which is composed of two characters, one representing danger and the other, opportunity. Politicians and motivational speakers have been dining out on the concept ever since. It does perfectly exemplify the concept of posttraumatic growth. In crisis, I did find growth. Just to survive the crisis, I *had* to grow. At UNC Charlotte, the Posttraumatic Growth Research Group Department of Psychology describes it this way:

"What is posttraumatic growth? It is positive change

experienced as a result of the struggle with a major life crisis or a traumatic event. Although we coined the term posttraumatic growth, the idea that human beings can be changed by their encounters with life challenges, sometimes in radically positive ways, is not new. The theme is present in ancient spiritual and religious traditions, literature, and philosophy. What is reasonably new is the systematic study of this phenomenon by psychologists, social workers, counselors, and scholars in other traditions of clinical practice and scientific investigation."
[ptgi.uncc.edu]

I see posttraumatic growth as yet another blessing of life with cancer to be celebrated. People from around the world have started emailing me for advice about healing naturally. This is not because I am a notable authority on the topic, but because I sometimes stick my nose in the territory of those who are new to the concept—online support groups for people with cancer and the like. They are frightened, terrified, really, suffering with all manner of side effects and chemo-generated illnesses. These groups I find heartbreaking. I have to speak up—gently, quietly, sort of a whisper as most of them are so deeply in Big Pharma's clutches, so frantically looking for the next nasty drug cocktail, the next fruitless clinical trial, they don't hear. I never tell them what they 'should do', (though I confess, I long to scream it out!) but rather point them to some resources (see The Asheville Protocol on my blog at julieparker.me to see what I did as well as my wish list) and suggest there are many things out there that can support their healing. And when relying on the power of Nature rather than the power of Big Pharma, everything we do will support our health. It is about deeply nurturing ourselves on all levels and detoxing on all levels: diet and lifestyle and relationships. Taking our health into our own hands, digging deep to unmask our true power is not for the faint of heart, but in my experience...

"If one advances confidently in the direction of his dreams, and

endeavors to live the life which he has imagined, he will meet with
a success unexpected in common hours."
Henry David Thoreau

Typically many people are wanting another choice, but express
some concern that they have not heard of anything that might
equal the "power" of chemo to heal. But I don't see it as a binary
choice. It is not one single thing, like chemotherapy vs. juicing, or
chemotherapy vs. whatever. It is about standing once your knees
have hit the floor and rolling up your sleeves and doing some
work: some reading, some googling, some seeking out others
who also want to heal with the power of nature. And it's about
using your intuition: tuning in deeply to your inner wisdom and
asking for guidance. It is about listening to your body, honoring it
and loving it and working with it to heal. It is not about going to
an infusion room, sticking out your arm for an IV and waiting for
the nausea to begin and your hair to fall out. It involves significant
doing on your part. It is about standing in your power. I guess you
could say that YOU are the power.

"I have loved the stars too fondly to be fearful of the night"
Galileo

"Your life is your story. Write well. Edit Often."
Ihadcancer.com

The relatively new exploration of post-traumatic growth is another
example of "everything old is new again". The concept has been
around for many centuries but has now been packaged for
popularity, to our benefit I believe. It is yet another way to 'flip the
script', a way to turn a curse into a blessing.

Post-traumatic growth (PTG) is not just about being glad to
be alive following a threat of dying. The official word on Post-
traumatic growth (PTG) from R.G. Tedeshi and L.G.Calhoun is:
"Post-traumatic growth (PTG) or benefit finding refers to positive

psychological change experienced as a result of adversity and other challenges in order to rise to a higher level of functioning." In contrast to resilience, hardiness, optimism, and a sense of coherence, post-traumatic growth refers to a change in people that goes beyond an ability to resist and not be damaged by highly stressful circumstances; it involves a movement beyond pre-trauma levels of adaptation."

In *Surviving Survival*, Laurence Gonzales says, "After major trauma, few people find an exact fit into the old way of life. And this means that you face the task of building a new life and, in some cases, as we'll see, even a new sense of who you are.."

CANCER AS CRUCIBLE
Merriam Webster's definition of CRUCIBLE:
1: a vessel of a very refractory material (as porcelain) used for melting and calcining a substance that requires a high degree of heat
2: a severe test
3: a place or situation in which concentrated forces interact to cause or influence change or development

Cancer can be our own trial by fire.

MY OWN TRAUMA
It was not just ovarian cancer and kidney cancer, but loss of my Work, loss of my beloved animals, loss of my home, loss of my ability to walk un-aided. For almost six years I struggled to find somewhere reliable I could live, twice literally preparing to move into my car. I still sometimes have challenges finding food at the end of the month when funds have run out.

MY OWN POST-TRAUMATIC GROWTH
So—cancer—how do I love thee? Let me count the ways: Without you, I would probably still be eating Cheetos. Without you, I would not have so mindfully chosen only the best personal care products

(often simple, basic things like coconut oil or baking soda). I would likely not have rid my life of a couple of toxic relationships. I would not have developed the habit of expressing gratitude everyday for everything, not a desperate plea to the gods for good fortune, but a natural, spontaneous joy that bubbles up and spills over. I would not have started seeing healing everywhere I look. I would not have had so many experiences of kindness and synergy and serendipity. I would probably still be living in a cave, curled up and nursing my wounds from the past. I would not have connected with so many wonderful new people. "Posttraumatic growth is facilitated by relating to others, new possibilities, personal strength, spiritual change, and appreciation for life."(Wikipedia)

Yes, it is a renewed appreciation for life since I had a bit of a brush with the alternative, but it is spiritual growth on steroids. All the right people and the right conversations and the right media are appearing at just the right time. I have begun to thrive. It is not that I never feel sadness or loss or loneliness, but there is a underlying hum of all-is-well in every moment.

Post-traumatic growth. Who knew it was a *thing?*

"When life knocks you down, roll over and look at the stars."
ralphsmart.com

In Which I Have Second Thoughts

"I'm sittin' here sucking down second thoughts."
Catherine Britt (*What I Did Last Night*)

Who am I to make all these pronouncements? I feel like I haven't even really experienced cancer. All my bodily processes continued unabated. I pee just fine with one kidney. I have had almost no pain (just a bit about 10 days after my nephrectomy). Because I am not poisoning myself with chemo, I have had no nausea and my hair is still firmly implanted in my scalp. I have not had septicemia, "mets" (metastases) to vital organs, chemo-brain, or any of the other nasties that can accompany chemotherapy, like lymphedema or neuropathy, so how dare I speak with any authority about having cancer?

I have the nerve to write a whole book about having cancer as if I could speak for all people with cancer. I have the nerve to upset so many people who have put their faith in the system. What if I am wrong? Some people I respect say that *sometimes*, *some* cancer patients can benefit from chemo. I really really doubt that, but... what if I am wrong?

Some people may strike out in anger about the things I have said. How will I endure that?

I have a couple of friends doing chemo.   I don't want them to read this—I don't want to undermine their belief in what they are doing.

Do I really want to expose some of my personal vulnerabilities to the world and even worse, to my friends and acquaintances who will read this book? I think I'd feel more comfortable if only strangers knew some of these things.

Does anyone even want to read this stuff? Will it be helpful to anyone?

What if the cancer comes back in a really ugly way—especially painful or debilitating?

Am I really unafraid of dying or will I panic at the last minute?

Am I going to die of cancer because I can't afford most of the things I should be doing to heal naturally (like eating organic all month long, like being able to afford the nuts and seeds I need and the organic supplements, or vitamin C therapy, infrared saunas, hyperbaric oxygen therapy, etc.)? And if I die from cancer, will people say, "See! Natural healing doesn't work. Her cancer killed her!" and I can't say "But, but, but, I couldn't afford the things I needed to do!"... because I will be dead.

Will dying hurt? What comes after death will be lovely, but the actual dying part—will that hurt?

I don't have anyone to be a caregiver—how will I die alone? Will someone find my decaying body days after I'm dead?

Will I ever have access to human touch before I die or will I live out my days with minimal, minimal human contact?

Yes, I am firm in my conviction that the path I have chosen is the only valid path for me, but... what if?

The Vocabulary of Joy

In Which I Dance with the D-word

*"To every thing there is a season, and a time to
every purpose under the heaven:
A time to be born, and a time to die; a time to plant,
and a time to pluck up that which is planted;"*
Ecclesiastes III

When my mother was in her last months, she'd say to her doctors with a grin "I'm not afraid of dying—I'm just not packed yet!"

Mother died with such grace and humor—she was an incredible role model for me. The director of Solace, the residential hospice where she spent her last 4 days, told me he'd never seen anyone die better. [On a side note, one of the nurses told me not everyone goes 'gentle into that good night': one woman angrily hit her call button again and again and when the nurse rushed into her room, she exclaimed with great disgust "Will someone get these damn angels OUT OF MY ROOM?!!"]

In contrast, an intuitive friend of mine visited Mother in her last days when she was drifting into the next world, and told me Mother was interviewing angels. I love that picture and can so envision her doing that. She probably said to them "Okay, so what's the scoop here? I'm ready—what's our plan?" Mother did not 'rage, rage against the dying of the light' nor did I on her behalf nor do I intend to when it is my turn to be 'plucked up'.

TAKING A CLOSER LOOK

Like most people, I expect, I always look away when having blood drawn. Now that I am dancing with cancer, having blood drawn is an all too frequent occurrence. One day recently I was sitting in my doctor's office, tourniquet wrapped tightly around my arm and needle sucking up my blood, when I decided to look. I wanted to confront head-on what I had steadfastly avoided watching all my life. And you know what? I didn't pass out or throw up. It was no biggie. I was so pleased with myself, I decided that I want to keep finding new things to do, things I'd been hesitant to face in the past. Now it is easy to watch the blood filling a tube—fascinating really, and I'm contemplating watching the needle actually go in next time. I even practiced watching a phlebotomy training video on youtube in preparation (and I neither 'winced nor cried aloud'.)

When I was in the hospital for the hysterectomy, I asked a CNA at one of my 2 a.m. check-ins if she would sit for a bit and tell me her experience with women dying of ovarian cancer—any she had witnessed—and bless her heart, she did. It was like watching the blood filling the tube, and I was at peace with it, even intrigued.

END OF LIFE CARE

"Everyone dies. Dying today typically involves a period of protracted illness, disability, and intense involvement of medical professionals. Although the experience is woefully understudied, a significant body of evidence is emerging to guide clinicians, health systems, and society toward better practices for people facing serious, life-threatening conditions."

Quantity and Quality of Life Duties of Care in Life-Limiting Illness
Atul Gawande, MD, MPH1
The Journal of the American Medical Association
[jama.jamanetwork.com]

In Which I Dance with the D-word

What fears motivate the desparate effort to stave off death at the expense of days/weeks/months lying in a diaper, in pain, and confusion? Death, like blood being sucked out of our bodies, is something many of us refuse to face head on. Do not take drastic measures to give me a few more weeks or months of misery! Please, do not artificially extend my life. Do not set up a 'deathwatch' in my last days/hours. You can come and visit from time to time, but know that I will be busy interviewing my own angels. Let my life, and my death, run its natural course.

A ROSE IS A ROSE IS A ROSE
Some people can't even say the word "die" — it is "passed" or "passed away" or "passed on" more often than not. Never a fan of euphemisms, I prefer "die". Neither the word nor the act scares me in the least. I have no fear of death nor do I fear the word "dying". I have no fondness for clichés and if I rage against anything, it is against the use of the word 'pass'. This is no criticism of folks who prefer it, but it does not sit well with me. The word 'death' to me only means the body is not up and walking around anymore. It doesn't mean anything about what comes next. So when my turn comes, please say Julie Parker DIED. Or that I croaked — I'd love to leave this world with a grin.

BLESSING # 37: A dear friend will serve as my death doula when the time comes. She knows the territory and is at peace with coming into the world and going out of the world. It is a tremendous honor that she has agreed to do this.

All life is cyclical, no? There is a time to 'lay down our burdens' — a time for deep, well-deserved rest. What a shame to meet that time with such fear and resistance! I am rather looking forward to (cliché warning) *making my transition*. It must feel lovely to (uh-oh, another one!) *pass* from the weight of the human experience to the infinite freedom of what comes next.

What exactly are you afraid of? The moment of death? What comes afterward? What you will miss after you are dead? There are so many ways to ease your fears if you still have them. You can ask to be guided to just what you need to reach a fuller understanding. There is so much out there to help—you are in for a serious googling session. Look for conscious dying, death doula, death cafe (deathcafe.com), NDE (near death experience). So many people have slipped over the edge a bit and come back totally free of fear! For example, you might want to read Anita Moorjani's book *Dying to Be Me*. From anitamoorjani.com:

> *"A near-death experience (NDE) refers to personal experiences associated with impending death, encompassing multiple possible sensations including detachment from the body, feelings of levitation, total serenity, security, warmth, the experience of absolute dissolution, and the presence of a light."*

The bonus with her book is that she had end stage cancer (Hodgkin's Lymphoma)—even a full-time nurse. After her near-death experience, she totally and quickly healed. That should inspire you!

FOOD FOR THE BELLY ... AND FOOD FOR THOUGHT
Why not savor the good stuff right now while you're still here? Something I enjoy doing when I eat is to deeply, deeply savor each bite of the food, thanking in my heart the person who prepared the ground and the person who sowed the seed and the sun and wind and rain that nurtured the plant and the soil itself and the earthworms and all the creatures that took part in the process (especially the honeybees!) who make it all possible, and the person who gathered the plant and then brought it to market and then the person who prepared it. The appearance of a single carrot from what was nothing to becoming part of your body is a sacred, magical journey. Mother Earth does this for us day after day after day. And then the vegetation dies back and is recycled in the bosom of the earth and is transformed and then blossoms again!

The Vocabulary of Joy

In Which I Dance with the D-word

You might have the opportunity to meet some farmers in your area who grew your food and thank them for their work. You might grow a garden of your own so you can experience each step from seed to your plate. Or if you have no garden, try growing something in your windowsill. I am a cilantro nut and love growing a pot of it in my 9th floor window. Growing at least a bit of your own food might help you ease into the rhythm. If you celebrate the wonder of what happens for us every day at every meal, I suspect you will not at the end of your life want to grasp hold of what was, but rather will lean back with a full belly of life and say "Yes, that was good!" And then *lean in* to your dying.

Google "mindfulness" if that is not already part of your life. Google "sadhana". Read deeply. Connect with others who understand these things.

BLESSING #14: GOOGLE itself! We have so much access to the body of human thought. (The good, the bad, and the ugly.)

Read the work of Bri Maya Tiwari and go to wiseearth.com.

Read about hospice and talk with some of your local hospice folk and see what they have to tell you about death and dying. Those I have met are such loving, peaceful people who understand there can be great beauty in the last days.

BLESSING #17: People and concepts and books and practices have been falling at my feet since I was diagnosed with cancer. It seems the whole universe has lined up and organized itself on my behalf. Say, "Universe, show me your stuff!" and it will.

Michael Newton's books are about his experiences learning about the "life between lives". [See SUGGESTED READING]

Are you afraid you won't see children and grandchildren grow up? My suspicion is that you will have a much better view from 'the other side'—leaving on earth all the fears and misgivings you may have now and knowing on a deep level that all is well.

Do you really think that what comes after life is not as full of abundant riches as our human experience? Why not much more so? How odd that death would be devoid of its own kind of splendor. I don't believe it for a minute!

BLESSING # 39: I live in Asheville where of course I have access to death doulas, of course there is a Death Cafe. [deathcafe.com] Asheville is not just a wonderful place to live, it is a wonderful place to die! Whitman reminds me of the magic and mystery of dying and how our culture denies it. I have yet to interview my friends who dance in this domain, (a domain that fascinates me) but for the last year we have been planning to get together one day to discuss it and it just hasn't happened yet. Perhaps in a future version of this book? Speaking of death, this is going to be a "living" book. That is, when you buy the book, email me your response to the book and I will send you a link to future online chapters, discussions,resources, etc. How does that sound?

TAKING DEATH INTO MY OWN HANDS
What about physician-assisted suicide/euthanasia? It is legal in all the left-coast states: Oregon, Washington, and California, as well as Montana and Vermont. I would be quite comfortable with that kind of help. I wish North Carolina would be added to the list! Whitman says there is such a thing as death tourists in Tijuana. I will have to look that up.

Yes, if I were in great pain, I would be quite open to a little help easing me over. And my doctor's humor and gentle manner would be just the ticket. I wonder what he would feel about 'putting me to sleep'? Which reminds me, when I had to have my dear Freya put to sleep in The-Year-From-Hell, 2010, I told my neighbor and she told her granddaughter who was most distressed. She asked "They didn't put Miss Julie to sleep too, did they?"

WRITING MY OWN OBITUARY

I happened to be reading the paper this morning (a very rare occurrence for me) and my eyes fell on the obituary page, and I actually read a few. Then I got excited about writing my own! I hope I have enough warning to do so. I attended my own funeral, why not write my own obituary?

JULIE SAVAGE PARKER - ASHEVILLE, NC

Julie Savage Parker, age TBA, finally croaked, ??/??/20??
Ms. Parker was born August 18, 1949 in Richmond, Virginia, daughter of Seth Thomas Parker and Irma Stevenson Parker. A funeral was held in 2013. Sorry you missed it. Ms. Parker was in attendance, and a good time was had by all. In lieu of flowers, buy *yourself* some flowers—frequently. Julie would love it if you surrounded yourself with them. Alas, *there were no survivors*, a source of deep sadness to Ms. Parker.

P.S. I am still working on the what-her-life-was-like part. A wonderful exercise!

AND THEN...

I saw a movie once where Robin Hood died, and they put his body on a small barge, surrounded him with flowers, and sent him out into the river. I'd love that! Or make a sweet bower entwined with flowers deep in the woods and lay me down there, and let me melt back into the earth.

MILEPOST 418.8

When my mother died, she left me with a gift I treasure: my cousin Katherine had come to be with me during what we were sure would be Mother's last days. For four days I mostly sat by her side at Solace, the residential hospice in Asheville. On what turned out to be Mother's last day, Katherine and I decided to go up on the Blue Ridge Parkway—it was May 22 and the day was beautiful. We headed up there in the very late afternoon, checking my

Celebrating the Blessings of Life with Cancer

cell phone everywhere we could pull off and get a signal, to see if hospice had called. When we pulled off at Milepost 418.8— ironically, Graveyard Fields—I checked in and the nurse said "Get back, now."

As we turned and headed back to Asheville, a beautiful golden/ pink cloud formation appeared in an otherwise cloudless sky, and then extended up at the top as if an arm was reaching to heaven.

On our return, we found Mother had already died. They'd warned me that people often choose to slip away when they are finally alone, and I was at peace with her choice. Katherine and I both felt she had clearly and lovingly said good-bye at Milepost 418.8.

[P.S. Katherine told me just the other day she thought Mother was not just saying goodbye, she was giving us the high sign. That would be just like Mother, to not wave a tearful farewell, but to rejoice in the journey leaving a dying human body to dance in the clouds.]

Qigong and Plant Spirit Medicine have both strengthened my connection with the earth and sky, and made it more porous. One day I may *be* that flock of birds that circles joyfully outside my window. I feel more and more a part of everything around me as if I could one day simply dissolve into it. Perhaps "transition" might be the best word after all.

I have already had my funeral (see *In Which I Attend My Own Funeral*) but if you really want to, it would be lovely to whisper the following words in my memory when you hear I'm at my own Milepost 418.8:

Do not stand at my grave and weep
I am not there. I do not sleep.
I am a thousand winds that blow.
I am the diamond glints on snow.

The Vocabulary of Joy

In Which I Dance with the D-word

I am the sunlight on ripened grain.
I am the gentle autumn rain.
When you awaken in the morning's hush
I am the swift uplifting rush
Of quiet birds in circled flight.
I am the soft stars that shine at night.
Do not stand at my grave and cry;
I am not there. I did not die.

Mary Elizabeth Frye

"

In Which I Go Deeply Into Debt

"Some people say a man is made outta' mud
A poor man's made outta' muscle and blood
Muscle and blood and skin and bones
A mind that's a-weak and a back that's strong

You load sixteen tons, what do you get?
Another day older and deeper in debt
Saint Peter don't you call me 'cause I can't go
I owe my soul to the company store"
Tennessee Ernie Ford

Medical expenses, according to a recent Harvard University study, account for approximately 62 percent of personal bankruptcies in the US. Count me in that number. Well, you could count me, but some years ago I had a complementary appointment with a bankruptcy attorney, only to find out I couldn't begin to *afford* to go bankrupt—the lawyer fees are way more than I could manage!

I "came down with" cancer a year before I "came down with" Medicare. Poor planning on my part, eh? And now I owe more than $64,000 to the company store—the $64,000 question, I suppose. Like how on earth can I even make a dent in that? Even a tiny fraction of a dent? The hospital even offered me an out— something about being a charity case. They offered that when

In Which I Go Deeply Into Debt

I was still in the hospital, but at that point I was still working on recuperating from six missing organs (and how do I fill up all that empty space?) and still trying to wash the lingering effects of anesthesia out of my mind/body. The stress of the debt threatened to knock me to my knees.

But really, at that point I was so worn down by three years of rather intense financial stress (preceded by a decade of semi-intense financial stress) even the charity case offer was overwhelming. Let's just say I have to look up, way up, to see the poverty line. I did attempt to gather the paperwork to satisfy their demands, but I kept missing the mark, kept screwing it up in one way or another. This morning in my writer's group, a friend and I got to talking about the shame that comes with poverty. Poverty is new to me, having grown up in a safely middle class family. Though as I think about it, when I was a child, my parents used to joke that we were living a life of 'genteel poverty'.

However my descent into this state happened (circumstance, karma, bad judgment on my part) I now struggle to get through the month covering the most basic of requirements. AND I need to come up with funds for healing, AND I have this humongous debt. I see friends posting photos of their meals on FACEBOOK and I dance between envy and anger (and wondering how this obsession with posting one's food got started). With me it is either feast or famine—literally. My friends never have to wonder where their next meal is coming from and they go on lovely holidays. What did I do so wrong? I do remember one friend talking about an acquaintance who was supporting herself with her writing. I had to challenge her on that. The writer is married, which means rent/mortgage is halved, utilities are halved, and while I have no idea what her financial circumstances are really (nor do I care), by sharing a roof, that takes a huge burden off one person. Another friend wanted a discount because she and her partner would have to buy two tickets. I thought, ohmigod, you pay *half* the living expenses a single person pays, and you want a *discount?!*

Yes, I do hear the bitterness and the self-pity. I do. The fact remains, a single person has a much harder time making ends meet—and sometimes you can only get them to meet with duct tape and chewing gum.

Anyway, single, married, or partnered, I am certainly not alone in facing enormous medical debt. I know mine is minuscule relative to what some others are facing. And this is not to rail against the system or the fates or the hospital or anyone/anything in particular. It is merely an observation of what is.

Eventually, in spite of the shame I felt, I 'womaned up' and called the hospital's billing department and threw myself on their mercy, explaining my situation and that I did not have a clue how I could pay my bill. The woman was lovely—she could not have been kinder. But, she said, we have already turned it over to collections.

For some time I spent many a sleepless night wondering how I could pay. I have finally moved beyond fretting about it, and have shifted to a sort of heck-with-them state and I am focused on subsistence living and occasionally a treat that will help me continue to heal. My friends and family have been most generous, but I so want them to be able to keep their money in their own pockets. How awful am I to be such a drag on their pocketbooks?

So I don't really have a moral-of-the-story here or any insightful conclusion. No ah-HA moments. Just what is...

In Which I Learn That Loneliness Kills

*"No matter what happens, whether the cancer
never flares up again or whether you die, the important thing is
that the days you have had you will have lived."*
Gilda Radner (SNL Comedian and Emmy Winner)

Gilda Radner died in 1989 of ovarian cancer. She was only 42. (I actually saw her on Broadway, back in the day.) Her death is probably the first time I ever gave any thought at all to ovarian cancer, though I doubt I had any premonition at the time of my own dance with the disease.

As I read her words, I think about what frightens me most about dying: in one way I will never have lived. I have never experienced love—as in "in love". (Gilda and Gene Wilder were deeply in love.) I have never created a baby with someone I loved. I don't remember ever even holding a baby (though I must have, surely, long ago.)

People tend to identify themselves in terms of relationship—sister, wife, mother, grandmother, aunt. I am none of those things. I have never been and never will be. In fact, I just filled out my request for absentee ballot form which said a near relative could request one on my behalf. "Near relative" was defined as spouse, brother, sister, parent, grandparent, child, grandchild, mother-in-law, father-in-law, daughter-in-law, son-in-law, stepparent, or stepchild. I am batting zero there. I do feel guilty sometimes when whining about having no family because I do have cousins, particularly my cousin Katherine who I feel so blessed to have in my life. But they live far away and I don't have any of the thirteen options above. Having none-of-the-above, I remain unidentifiable, drifting unattached and alone in the cold vastness of space. Melodramatic and self-pitying I know, yes? But I have been through two cancers and my brain going haywire in the past several years, and no one has once just held me, or even held my hand.

Oh my.... I just checked Facebook and there was a Prince Ea video that stated, *"It is not death most people are afraid of. It is getting to the end of life only to realize that you never truly lived."* Oh yes. Just my point.

Judith Shulevitz wrote an article in the May 13, 2013 issue of *New Republic* entitled *"The Lethality of Loneliness: We now know how it can ravage our body and brain"*. She says:

> *"In a way, these discoveries are as consequential as the germ theory of disease. Just as we once knew that infectious diseases killed, but didn't know that germs spread them, we've known intuitively that loneliness hastens death, but haven't been able to explain how. Psychobiologists can now show that loneliness sends misleading hormonal signals, rejiggers the molecules on genes that govern behavior, and wrenches a slew of other systems out of whack. They have proved that long-lasting loneliness not only makes you sick; it can kill you."*

I had no idea that there is a strong link between cancer and loneliness and death until my primary care doctor brought it up in my first appointment after cancer surgery. I had asked my two

The Vocabulary of Joy

dear friends (and Health Care Power of Attorney people) to come with me for a sort of state-of-Julie appointment. My doctor told me (he knows me pretty well) that Job #1 for me was to reconnect with people. If you do a web search on loneliness and cancer, you will find an abundance of material. He knew I had been living in a cave, curled up licking my wounds. But at that point in my cancer journey I admit to being surprised at his 'prescription'.

Then as we were leaving, my doctor gave me a lovely hug. My friend Julia N asked me as we were walking out the door why I had looked so uncomfortable. I was startled that I'd looked in any way uncomfortable because on the surface I had been thinking, "What a nice surprise!" But since it had just happened, I was able to do a sort of instant replay of my interior monologue: "Oh, it has been so long since I have been touched by another human, especially a man human. When will it happen again? Probably a long, long time, if ever," complete with quivering lower lip. My next thought was "Am I doing it right? Is my nose facing in the right direction? Are my hands where they are supposed to be? My arms?" And finally "Let go, Julie! Let go! Don't be clingy, don't be desperate! How many seconds is too long to hug?" I really wanted so to just hold on a bit, to feel someone's kindness and good wishes, and to simply feel the warmth of another human body. Just for a moment. So the hug was sort of 'best of times, worst of times' thing, but of course it was I who made it that way by my own loneliness and insecurity.

Facebook is especially painful for me as people tend to parade their husbands/spouses/lovers, children, and grandchildren, nieces and nephews (NONE of which I have) in beaming group shots, touching, touching, touching... There are always, it seems, shots of people with their heads bending towards each other. Why do they have to do that when someone pulls out a camera? Do they do that at any other time in their life, or only on camera? Is there something wrong with me that my head remains unbent?

SKIN HUNGER

"We are not people who touch each other carelessly; every point of contact between us feels important, a rush of energy and relief."
Veronica Roth, *Allegiant*

Sharon K Farber, Ph.D. in *The Mind-Body Connection: Why We All Need to Touch and Be Touched*, Psychology Today, September 11, 2013:

> *"Being touched and touching someone else are fundamental modes of human interaction, and increasingly, many people are seeking out their own "professional touchers" and body arts teachers – chiropractors, physical therapist, Gestalt therapists, Rolfers, the Alexander technique and Feldenkrais people, massage therapists, martial arts and T'ai Chi Ch'uan instructors. And some even wait in physicians' offices for a physical examination for ailments that have no organic cause—they wait to be touched."* [Emphasis mine]

My hunger/thirst for touch is so intense, I get a thrill from holding my hands under running water—cold, warm, hot—I don't care. I love wind and even breeze from a fan. Any form of touch. Did I manifest this cancer just so I could be touched? I have sat in the offices of my gyn/oncologist, my urologist, my nephrologist, my gastrointerologist, my primary care doc... always waiting, hoping, longing to be touched.

I really don't know if I can heal without the touch of another human. I would be happy if each of my doctors would gently put his or her hand on my arm and just rest it there. That would be the most healing thing they could do for me. Twenty minutes of human contact—I'd gladly pay for that! Just sitting quietly and being able to breathe it in... and not worrying about my nose.

I can pay someone to touch me. I can afford a massage a couple of times a year. Massage is lovely, but it is a one-way street—we are not allowed to touch back. We crave touching as well as being touched. What long-term stress is this putting my body through, having neither? Right now I have a little lump on the back of my knee but I don't know if it is supposed to be there. I have no idea what other people's knees feel like. Am I going to die without ever feeling anyone's knees? Without ever again being held? I don't mean a brief hug. Hugs are few and far between, but even if I had one every week, it is a quick-squeeze-and-let-go. And I have them more like once a month, if then. Human touch is critical to thriving, if not surviving. How can I heal without human touch? Can I heal—is it even possible?

I used to love the warmth of dog bodies. At one time I had three of them, and they never cared which way my nose was pointing or if I held on "too long". It doesn't look like I will ever be able to have a dog again.

Someone just posted this on Facebook: *"On the road of life, it is not where you go but who you're with that makes the difference."* And if you are with no one, do you not 'count'? You see everywhere that family is the most important thing in life. And if you don't have one? At Christmas time I allow my buttons to be pushed rather easily, everytime someone sends best wishes to "you and yours". When my nerves are raw, I want to scream "I don't have a @#$! 'yours'!" I find it outrageous that they assume the "yours". Then I calm down and just appreciate the kind wishes.

Shulevitz in *The New Republic* again:
> *"What's most momentous about the new biology of loneliness is that it offers concrete proof, obtained through the best empirical means, that the poets and bluesmen and movie directors who for centuries have deplored the ravages of lonesomeness on both body and soul were right all along. As W. H. Auden put it, 'We must love one another or die.'"*

Celebrating the Blessings of Life with Cancer

I can eat my green leafies and turmeric until the cows come home, but I cannot manifest human contact. Will lack of touch prove deadly to me?

"Healing is impossible in loneliness; it is the opposite of loneliness. Conviviality is healing. To be healed we must come with all the other creatures to the feast of Creation."
(pg.99, "The Body and the Earth")
Wendell Berry, *The Art of the Commonplace: The Agrarian Essays*

I wrote the following in 2002, long before the arrival of cancer, and it might paint a clearer picture. (There is a tiny bit of blurring details as this was published locally.)

in praise of casual intimacy
by julie parker

They told me I could tell you about my fantasies. They said I could describe in vivid detail who touched what where, and it would be okay. So I will.

'He pressed against me with all his might as I struggled to break free' . . . 'She held me in her arms and didn't let go, as the fire rose and the drumbeat quickened' . . . 'Our eyes met and he ran towards me, arms wide, calling my name again and again' . . .

I don't want to disappoint you, but nothing throbbed and nothing moistened. And the only thing that grew warm was my heart.

He pressed against me with all his might as I struggled to break free: He was 10 at the time, and sitting next to me in a booth in a restaurant where I was visiting his family. When I tried to slip out to pick up my juice, he leaned into me, keeping me captive in my corner of the booth, giggling and wiggling in the way a ten year old does best. He kept up a steady pressure against me, determined I wouldn't leave. I leaned back, exhilarated, savoring the most human contact I had had in six months. I love this kid and his brother; horsing around with them is one of my greatest pleasures. It was his brother who ran towards me, arms wide, calling my name again and again the day they met me at the airport. "Oolijay! Oolijay!" (I had taught them Pig Latin.)

These kids are the children of friends of mine, sort of nephews of the heart, and the time I spent with them was one of my greatest joys. It was their mom who held me in her arms and didn't let go as we hugged one night around a bonfire and drumming. It was not one of those five-second hugs, but a hug that was just about holding on, loving, and slipping out of time. I am a heterosexual woman as is she, yet being in this woman's arms was an intensely pleasurable (totally non-sexual) experience.

These are examples of what I call casual intimacy.

The longing for this kind of intimacy for those without access to loved ones' touch is intense. Imagine being very thirsty and having to wait hours to drink, or very tired and having to stand for hour after hour without a moment to sit down. Eventually, you will be able to drink, and to sit. Gratification is delayed, but the delay is still finite. When you don't have access to touch, the longing—the thirst, if you will—is accompanied by the knowledge that *there is no eventual gratification*—just an endless, aching need. The everyday sort of touch—a squeeze when passing, a bit of horseplay, a child curled up in your arms as you are reading to her, a hug good morning, or the bump of a familiar stray body part in a warm bed—all of it becomes the stuff of daydreams, of fantasies forever unfulfilled. 'Casual intimacy' is non-sexual touch between any two people who care for each other, no matter the age, gender, or relationship.

When you measure body-to-body human contact in seconds, spaced days, weeks, or even months apart, fantasies tend towards the gentle touch of anyone you care for. Well yes, the throbbing, arching, 'age-old rhythm', yes, yes, YES! fantasies still exist, but all-in-all play second fiddle to the yearning for casual intimacy. Men, women, or children—it doesn't matter. It only needs to be loving family or family-of-the-heart.

Going Postal

My friend Dill and I sometimes compare notes. "How are you doing?" we ask, which is shorthand for "How are you managing? Have you run screaming into the streets yet? Have you 'gone postal'?" as my friend Alyssa threatens to do from time to time when she's at the end of her rope. Ours is a hurried, almost whispered conversation, as if we were sharing some kind of shameful secret. How are you managing to survive, much less thrive when you are missing that aspect of life which is so very precious? That is the undercurrent of our question.

There is a continuum of isolation . . . Dill and I are at the far end, being without spouse, parents, brothers, sisters, children—all of which makes in-laws, nieces, nephews, and grandchildren somewhat problematic. Most of my friends have children, some have a lover or a spouse, and others have the full complement of loved ones—the regulation husband, kids, and family dog. There are a few of us who 'understand'. The rest don't have a clue.

Some are quick to label those of us on the far end of the touch-deprivation spectrum as co-dependent when we express an intense need for loving connection. New Age moralizing holds that we should be totally sufficient unto ourselves, without need for human touch or companionship.

The Vocabulary of Joy

We are told by these same people that "we are spiritual beings having a human experience". Yes indeed. That means we have the requisite flesh, blood, bones, and NEEDS of a HUMAN. We were meant to live in a pack. We are meant, from time to time, to glory in the pile-of-puppies kind of contact that is warm, intimate, and totally without sexual content—the kind that is virtually nonexistent when you have no family.

Death by Deprivation

Isolation kills. The rates of depression and suicide are highest among people living alone. Though the elderly (in 1997) were only 13% of the population, they were 19% of the suicide rate. I have long felt that touch deprivation has a chemical component—as if it were some sort of vitamin that is necessary for healthy functioning. Lack of this 'vitamin' has serious consequences, one of which is clearly depression. Otherwise healthy people, otherwise happy people whose lives are going well, when they have their whispered, furtive conversations with those who understand, admit that a lifetime without casual intimacy is untenable, and suicide as an alternative sometimes takes on a rosy glow.

The Touch Hormone

Seems ol' Dr. Phil has been on Oprah again, and he was talking about the relationship between touch and oxytocin. It turns out there is an abundance of information about the hormone and its connection with touch, women, and depression. Aha! I thought. I knew there was a 'vitamin' related to touch, and I knew it was absolutely critical to sustain life. Babies can die without touch *and so can adults*.

I am convinced that the touch of one's own child—rocking a baby in our arms, holding a baby to our breast, washing jellied faces and wiping snotty noses—can give us a supercharged dose of touch 'vitamins'. Those of us who have had not even one moment of this touch have a massive deficiency that can have a profound effect on our development as human beings.

Here's what I've found out from the research:
(1) Physical touch boosts oxytocin levels in the body
(2) Oxytocin promotes feelings of affection and well-being
(3) There is a direct connection between human touch and protection from disease
(4) Without physical closeness, the full range of love is restricted
(5) Touch is a better antidepressent than pharmaceutical drugs
(6) Absence of touch promotes depression and aggression
(7) Touching, holding close, snuggling are critical to health—especially to the health of the heart
(8) Oxytocin plays a role in women's higher levels of depression and interpersonal stress
(9) A close, regular relationship influences the responsiveness of the oxytocin

Tend and Befriend
What they have finally realized is that it is men, not women, who have a "fight or flight" response. Women have an entirely different response to stress—we need to "tend or befriend". Women have a deep, primal need to nurture in times of stress. We have an actual chemical need to connect with people we love. When women are denied this contact, our stress level can rise as high as sixty percent; blood pressure goes up; fatigue sets in. A myriad of stress-induced ailments are just around the corner. Beri-beri is the result of a B1 deficiency; scurvy is the result of a C deficiency, etc. Clinical depression, I suggest, may in many cases be the result of lack of touch.

"I Wish I Were an Oscar Meyer Wiener"
Temple Grandin—diagnosed at two with autism—is now Professor of Livestock Behavior & Welfare at Colorado State University, and an expert designer of humane facilities for livestock animals. She created squeeze chutes and restraint

systems that prevent animals from being hurt and that also keep them calm. She built a similar device for herself, she said, "(1) to help relax my "nerves" and (2) to provide the comforting feeling of being held." She goes on to speak of the neurological damage caused by withdrawal from touching: "The machine provides comforting pressure to large areas of the body. One day about 12 years ago, a Siamese cat's reaction to me changed after I had used the squeeze machine. This cat used to run from me, but after using the machine, I learned to pet the cat more gently and he decided to stay with me. I had to be comforted myself before I could give comfort to the cat..."

"Therapists have found that deep pressure stimulation has a calming effect.", from *An Inside View of Autism Temple Grandin, Ph.D.*

Grandin continues: "In the fourth grade, I was attracted to election posters because I liked the feeling of wearing the posters like a sandwich man. Occupational therapists have found that a weighted vest will often reduce hyperactivity."

Yes! Me too! At the dentist recently, about to have a tooth pulled, I wanted to wear the heavy vest they'd put me in when doing the x-rays . . . its firm pressure against my body was the kind of comfort I craved while my tooth was on its way out. I wanted to take the vest home with me and wear it all the time. My longing for pressure against my body—a kind of "hug"—is so intense that I my keep bed pushed alongside the wall so I can press against it at night for comfort, even when the wall radiates nothing but a mid-winter chill.

I can see myself in Grandin's device, being held for an hour or so every day, like a 5'2" hotdog in a giant bun. Without sexual touch, women are left to their own, uh, devices. Without non-sexual touch, perhaps what we need is our own squeeze machine, our own non-sexual pleasure device to hold us, comfort us, when we have no other options. What are we to do, those of us who are 'oxytocin-challenged?' Do we call up Temple Grandin, order our own squeeze machine, and become giant human hotdogs?

...Please pass the mustard!

First published in WNC WOMAN magazine, July 2003

WHITMAN STRIKES AGAIN

My body is tight and my breath shallow. Whitman said I have not revealed *why* I have been so isolated and the reader will be left puzzled and unfulfilled. I sent a reply email telling him why I thought that might be the case—the very very personal sort of email one might write after having one too many beers. The thing is, I don't drink beer.

Whitman replied: *"Julie, thank You for being so open and courageous and trusting little old me with your very personal stuff. I feel very honored. My suggestion: include this email response to me in your book. That would do it. Get some rest. You deserve it. Talk soon. w "*

I almost left this whole chapter out, and now he wants me to dig even deeper! I didn't have any idea when I started this book that I would be in for a 'big reveal'. Okay, I am taking a deep breath and jumping off the cliff:

I am not 100% sure of the reasons WHY I am so isolated. Part is the weight. I was a normal size until after college and then, like Alice, I started getting bigger and bigger and bigger (though in my case rounder and rounder.) The last time I had a "date", kiss, sex, etc. was senior year in college. Nineteen seventy-two. How does one explain or even understand that? The conventional

The Vocabulary of Joy

wisdom on that is that there was likely some sexual abuse in my past, but as far as I know, there wasn't. I am a perfectly healthy heterosexual woman (okay, I guess with two cancers, not so much, but you get my point) with the same needs and desires as anyone else, even at 66. I had no siblings (hence no brothers, no nephews) and my father died when I was 13 so there has been almost no male energy in my life. I dated some nice guys but I was only sexually active the last two years of college, and then not really, well, "active". The male I was closest to I dated the last two years of high school and the first two of college, but we never had sex. I appreciate that the few men I dated in college were good people but I was too shy to be 'physically outgoing', I guess you could say. I saw the cover of a novel the other day where a woman was sitting with a man with his arm around her, comfortably resting her hand on his thigh. I don't think I ever had that experience. There was kissing and making out and sex, yes, but no 'casual intimacy', no resting my hand on any body part at any other time. It was the early 70s (a time of burgeoning sexual liberation) but I was rather shy and came close to missing the boat entirely.

One of the three to whom the book is dedicated – my dear friend Diane Douglas, the OT who does the integrative manual therapy, wonders if I am not hiding in the weight but rather reaching out... my body is expanding to find something to touch, to hold. There was a tiny 1/2" worm-like thing the other day that appeared on a sheet of paper by my chair. It had reached the edge of the paper and was feeling all around in the air for the next thing to grab hold of... reaching its tiny little blind body everywhere and finding nothing. It was heart-breaking. I finally connected him with another piece of paper. I have no idea where he is now. Sometimes I feel like that tiny little creature, reaching out in vain for something to touch, to hold, to connect with.

I had an interesting stint of male touch the six months before I moved in here. While I was waiting for my name to rise to the top of the waiting list, a man (a friend of a friend) I'd never even met opened his home to me. He is a gay man and very open with his feelings and gave me lovely hugs right from the beginning. Eventually I got up my nerve and gave him hugs sometimes too. His friends would come around (90% gay) and I got to be friends with them too. I had so much fun spending six months in a house full of wonderful, kind, happy men! At last, some time before I die, I had time under the same roof as a lovely man—one I could touch. Well, hug, anyway.

For comic relief: I learned just a couple of years ago that men can pee sitting down. I know so little about men, I had no idea.

Anyway, I got down to ??? lbs at the onset of cancer because with zero appetite (one symptom of ovarian cancer) I lost weight. Now I have ballooned up to ??? lbs, probably the biggest I have ever been. In the middle of the night last night I got a "message" that much of the flesh I am wearing now is inflammation. Not that I didn't know it before, but it really hit home. "It's the inflammation, stupid!" is more or less what I heard, and then relief like good grief, we've been trying to get this message through to you for SO LONG. And inflammation is a serious precursor to cancer, so I have my work cut out for me.

When I was forced out of my Work in 2010, there went SO MUCH human contact, at least relative to now... writers, subjects of articles, advertisers, people who attended the conferences we put on. And the phone for the mag rang at my house so WHOOSH! all that contact was gone. So I curled up in a ball and whimpered. That was when I was evicted (because my rent started being late every month, though I always paid by the end of the month) and two of my dogs died and I thought I was going to have to move into my car with my last dog IN THE SUMMER and my blood pressure went up to 280/160 and my brain started bleeding. When I think back to those days I can hardly breathe. Everything that could go wrong, did.

In Which I Learn That Loneliness Kills

I have buried this 'confession' at the tail end of a long chapter, and I can only hope that the reader has long since gotten bored and moved on to another chapter or put the book down for a while and then lost their place. Ohmygod, I actually wrote my weight!! My most shameful secret. Well, I have time to go back and take that part out.

Ironically, I learned that two old boyfriends now live in the area... one about 20 minutes east of here, and one 20 minutes west. The one to the east was my very last date, 43 years ago. (If I were a character in a novel, I would not believe me.) I live in terror that I will run into them one day, but hang onto the belief that they could not possibly recognize me.

Weight is a high risk factor for cancer. In my case, it has been largely responsible for my strange, lonely life, and we know that loneliness is also a huge risk factor for cancer. If I didn't have so much going for me in other areas, I'd swear I was doomed. Flip the script, Julie! Re-write the ending of your life.

So... why did I choose to bare my soul to the world in this overwhelmingly anxiety-producing way you may be wondering. Well—if you take nothing else from this—this is actually my core message. I think loneliness and isolation related to loss led to my cancer. Weight contributed to this, adding to the cancer... and yet the cancer itself is what "cured" the isolation and loneliness, by bringing me back into contact other other humans. By forcing dependence, it forced connection. Connection brought relationship, relationships brought love... and the vocabulary of joy.

In Which The Cancer Comes Back

"When you have exhausted all possibilities,
remember this: You haven't."
Thomas Alva Edison

Well dang. It came back—or maybe not. My oncologist says that ovarian cancer doesn't typically spread to the kidney (though mine was the third she had seen in the last 6 years). Anyway, just before Thanksgiving last year (2015) they found a tumor in my right kidney, situated right on top of grand central station of arteries and things. It would be too complicated/ dangerous to try to pick around all that and just get the tumor, so they had to pop out the whole kidney. The good news is that because the tumor was smack dab in the middle of the kidney, removing it meant no further treatment—no chemo— was necessary. But whether it spread or just coincidentally chose my body in which to appear, I am so fortunate that I had the foresight to have a spare.

Is it then coincidence that a person has two unrelated cancers? Who knows? And what about the "primary" cancer they never found? My urologist (the doc who removed the kidney) said when he got in there, he thought it looked like it was about to blow— about to start traveling through the bloodstream to reach foreign shores. I was grateful my primary care doctor was on top of things and sent me to a urologist in time.

The Vocabulary of Joy

In Which The Cancer Comes Back

It just occurs to me that I don't like the word *remission*. Suddenly I feel the need to dig into the dictionary definition to be certain I understand its full implications: okay, the dictionary says it is a *temporary* recovery. The synonyms are *respite* and *abeyance*. Abeyance is a state of *'temporary* disuse or suspension'. I am not happy with the dictionary. I am not really wild about this 'temporary' stuff. My oncologist, by the way, never actually told me I was in remission. I had to ask. (I wonder if she was resisting acknowleging how well I did without the chemo she wanted me to have.) On my online ovarian cancer support group, they use the term NED–no evidence of disease– which apparently is the same thing, but to me sounds better. *Remission* sounds like it is lurking in the back alleys of my belly, ready to pounce.

My cancerversary is in September so I have been in remission/ NED for three years. Five years is the magic number. If you make it to five years, you are considered more or less in the clear. I think I will throw a party two years from now. I might write a sequel to this book if I have the good fortune to be my own sequel in two years. A deeper look, however, shows that recurrence after 5 years is still possible. I think after five years they just quit counting and pat themselves on the back. I wonder if 5 years is really a rather arbitrary number...

Am I afraid of it happening again, of new cancer showing up? Well, I do feel it is best to keep the rest of my original equipment. Might something happen one day cancer-wise and I feel fear? Yes, of course. Especially if I start having problems with an organ that is not really optional. In fact, at the moment my gall bladder is complaining, one night so much so that I unlocked my door and sat with my phone in my hand to be ready in case the pain got significantly worse. It did. I finally called 911 and they came and got me, but by the time I'd arrived in the hospital and they started poking me, I was feeling significantly better. They kept me for three days anyway (no complaints here). It seems that if a gallstone is finding its way out, in can get stuck in a potentially deadly spot. Am I worried about that? Well, there is nothing I can do about it so that worry is on the back burner. Have I started seeing cancer lurking with every twinge, every mole that changes color/shape/size? Well, no but... last year I did have a thing on my arm that radically changed color rather suddenly. It had a rough surface and went from pale pink to a liver color. I contacted Dr. Lewis who could tell I was somewhere between a bit concerned and slightly panicky. He said come in and just show me in the waiting room. I was there within the hour, and when he popped his head out between patients I just held out my arm, determined to say nothing to take a minute more of his time than necessary. He took one look, grinned kindly and said, "It's not cancer." I felt a bit like I had gone to mama with a booboo and she had reassured me in that oh so comforting way that I would be okay. This is a doctor who has earned his brownie points, by allowing me to come in on a day he was jam-packed and come up with the clever idea to let me hold out my arm in the waiting room. Fears allayed, dragons slain.

NURSE IN SHINING ARMOUR

Anyway, back to my kidney. Surgery was smooth and went more quickly than expected. This time around I had read a book by Peggy Huddleston called *Prepare for Surgery, Heal Faster*. Huddleston strongly encourages having a person stay with you the first 24-48 hours. That had never occurred to me for the hysterectomy 3 years ago, where I waited for three hours alone in pre-op and returned to an empty room from post-op. Since I have no immediate family and I am used to doing all of my medical things alone. It never occurred to me there was another option.

This time my sweet friend T volunteered to show up for me when I had the nephrectomy. She arrived early in the morning to drive me to the hospital and then spent the night as well, doing her best to sleep in the not-very-comfortable recliner in my room. She even saw me through part of the next day. It was such fun to have a

The Vocabulary of Joy

friend along, especially because she was not distraught about what was happening, but calm and joked happily with me before and after. And the bonus? T is a nurse! So she really knew what she was doing. I am deeply moved by her doing this. An hour's visit from a friend when you are in the hospital means so much, but her visit was more than 24 hours.

MUSIC TO MY EARS

My dear friends Herb and Karen sent me an MP3 player to fill with healing music for me to listen to (with headphones) during surgery, also recommended by Huddleston. She explains that hearing persists, even when you are unconscious, and operating rooms are noisy, she says (I wonder why). She also warned that the surgeon may say something disturbing/frightening that you are actually on some level hearing, so I decided I wanted to be cocooned in a cloud of gentle healing music. Gentle, healing music for me is anything by Peter Kater, R. Carlos Nakai, Paul Horn, or any combination of the three. I threw in Paul Potts' Nessun Dorma for good measure, a sprinkling of Loreena McKennitt, a dash of Scott Sheerin, and believe it or not, Dobie Gray's *Drift Away* ("Oh, give me the beat boys and free my soul / I wanna get lost in your rock and roll and drift away"). That one always knocks my socks off. Okay, and I put a few of my favorite Beatles in (*Yesterday, Let it Be*). Two more that always thrill me to my toes: almost any version of Leonard Cohen's *Hallelujah*, (K.D. Lang's especially) and the Poozies' *Another Train*. [Find *Another Train* on youtube and listen. I predict you will come out sockless.] I am not sure how I missed Simon and Garfunkel, but I did. My dear friend Lisa helped load me up with healing CDs, and I even added some 'post-hypnotic' suggestions of my own to the mix (some habits I wanted to break, some I wanted to establish) just in case that kind of thing might work when under anesthesia.

LALA LAND

For the surgery in 2013 they had given me a drug called Versed (alias Midazolam) prior to wheeling me into the OR to calm me down, but as I have been meditating for the last 44 years, I was plenty calm without being drugged. Versed causes retrograde amnesia so I had no memory of them coming to get me (though I clearly remembered lying there for hours by myself) or giving me the Versed or entering the OR or anything. The first thing I remember was waking up in post-op with the nurse saying *Breathe! Breathe! Breathe!* (I always wondered was there an issue with my breathing, or is that just something they say routinely to help patients wake up.) I felt a bit cheated because I really wanted to enjoy the whole operating room experience. I mean, how often do you get to have major surgery? Okay, so in my case, twice so far, but at the time, I didn't know a second major surgery was on the horizon.

For the nephrectomy (removing my kidney—cancer brings with it a significant growth in one's vocabulary) I told them "Please don't give me Versed—I want to remember this!" Versedless, I was able to look around an actual operating room. I felt like I was a guest star in *Grey's Anatomy* and I had no fear because I had *written my own script*. It was great fun kidding around with the OR staff. The name tag of one of the women standing over me was flipped (have you ever noticed their nametags are so often flipped so you only see the blank backside?) I told her (with a grin) that I wanted to know her name in case something went terribly wrong in the operation, and without missing a beat she said "Throckmorton", the name of the anesthesiology (male) nurse across the table. Not only did kidding around with them keep me totally relaxed, but I assume operating on someone they had just been goofing around with would relax them too. I enjoyed meeting the people who were going to be poking around in my insides, seeing parts of me I will never see.* I wished they'd film the operation so I could see

*Now about female genitals—that is something I will never get to see (and a mirror doesn't really cut it). Being neither a doctor or a lesbian (or rather more adventurous than I tend to be) I never will. But there is that absolutely critical part of me that is totally unknown to me. How bizarre that other people can see us much more clearly than we can see ourselves! "O wad some Power the giftie gie us. To see oursels as ithers see us!" ~ from Robert Burns' poem, "To A Louse, On Seeing One on a Lady's Bonnet at Church"

The Vocabulary of Joy

it later. (In preparation for the surgery, I had watched a laproscopic nephrectomy on youtube.) I relished the adventure, and part of me wished for a flashy near-death experience, though I expect that would certainly have freaked out the surgical team. But perhaps I'd wake up with acquired savant syndrome due to some medical error in surgery, and suddenly I'd be able to speak fluent Chinese or be a concert pianist or sing opera. Or shoot—dance!

IT ISN'T MUNCHAUSEN'S—I SWEAR!
I experienced tremendous warmth and kindness with the two stays in the hospital, particularly the first one which was more of a big deal (removal of 6 organs instead of just the 1) and a longer stay in the hospital. In fact, since I have been alone almost 24/7 for so many years, I have to say I really loved my time in the hospital. I wouldn't mind going back, but I think I may have just about run out of optional organs.

Munchausen's Syndrome, if you have not come across it on a TV medical drama, is when someone essentially seeks medical treatment and/or admission to a hospital for no physical reason. According to the Cleveland Clinic, two of the symptoms I can relate to:

- Willingness or eagerness to have medical tests, operations, or other procedures
- More comfortable being in the hospital than you might think

While I don't invent issues for operations or hospital stays, I really was excited to have another operation that I could experience without amnesia this time, and I did enjoy my hospital stay. My friends wonder if I am a bit nuts. But hospitals offer more opportunities for touch (even if needles are sometimes included) and more opportunities for meeting people and conversations, even if brief. This is either pitiful on my part or highly adaptive... or a smattering of each? And even beyond touch, at a certain point in my life after years of being without any human arms in which to find a bridge over trouble waters, as it were, it was a relief to rest for a while in the metaphorical arms at least of a group of people dedicated to my comfort and well-being. They were there, 24/7, always saying "Let us know if we can do anything for you." Most people seemed to think "Poor Julie, she has to be in the hospital. She has to have surgery." But I was having a fine time.

Humans are an interesting bunch, aren't we? We have such a wide range of responses to things. Someone in my support group observed the other day that when you are going 'all natural', people tend to forget you are dealing with cancer and go on about their business as if we no longer need their 'it takes a village' kind of support. There may be some truth to that. No matter how well I am doing, I am still aware that I am dancing with cancer and must remain vigilant. I wonder if on some level I welcomed the second cancer as if to say "See—I still need your love and attention!" Introspection is a daily dance when engaging in mind/body/spirit healing.

Actually, since I have lived in Asheville, I have been in the hospital *five* times (and never before). Five times—it startles me to count them all up. The first was in the year from hell, 2010, when my 'head exploded' (blood pressure as high as 280/160; the second, a serious attack of gout that they misdiagnosed at first and prepared me for surgery the next morning; the third, the hysterectomy; the fourth, the nephrectomy; the fifth, three days in the hospital to find the source of severe abdominal pain in the middle of the night. (I can't help it: I enjoyed the ambulance ride through downtown Asheville when most of the town was sound asleep.) They never found the source of the pain though they suspect it was a gall bladder attack and flirted with the idea of popping it out. That would be eight organs. Okay, to be fair, I am counting two ovaries and two Fallopian tubes. But they are my organs and I get to count them that way if I want.

The truth is, I did not particularly fear the kidney cancer appearing,

The Vocabulary of Joy

but I know at the moment I am chock full of inflammation. Chronic inflammation increases cancer risk as does my weight as does my lack of mobility, now that my balance has forced me to rely on a walker. So it is the perfect storm, at least that is how I sometimes see it in the wee hours of a sleepless night. My work is definitely cut out for me. But my doctor has just the right moves in dealing with me. In my last visit I was fretting about what might be filling me up and I was speculating about what could be rattling around inside me. I was listing to him: "fat, ascites, inflammation, lymph, water, gas..." and without missing a beat he picked up the list: "liver, kidney, lungs, heart..."

BACK TO THE NEPHRECTOMY

The details of my surgeries are not important except to encourage those facing surgery to breathe easy and enjoy the trip to lala land and back. It is a good time to "flip the script"—a term I recently heard on an NPR report. I decided to flip the script on surgery; instead of fearing it, dreading it, I laughed with it and saw it as an adventure. It is clear that our attitude makes a huge contribution to our healing from the experience. And we can flip the script on cancer too. It worked for me, anyway.

In Which I Find the Cure for Cancer

*"Our society has a magic bullet fixation, waiting
for the next miracle drug to cure us of every ill."*
Deepak Chopra

*"Instead of thinking outside of the box,
get rid of the box."*
Deepak Chopra

*"When you have a disease, do not try to find a cure.
Find your center and you will be healed."*
The Yellow Emperor's Classic of Internal Medicine,
a book written circa 400 b.c.

The cure for cancer does NOT lie in Big Pharma's labs, so let's quit looking there. Actually, I don't see that the cure for anything lies in Big Pharma's labs, so let's stop pouring money into that lost cause. The cure has really been in front of our noses all the time. We need to go beyond Turmeric vs. Tamoxifen, chemo vs. cauliflower—way beyond. The cure for cancer goes far beyond a single bullet, chemical or natural. The issue is not just a cluster of cells that have gone haywire, but rather finding ourselves out of balance and harmony not only within body or within our spirit, but within the fabric of life as a whole. We need to come home to our center.

In Which I Find the Cure for Cancer

BRASS TACKS
A reminder that this is a living book—there is a rich list of resources that will continue to grow. Email me at julie@handwovenwebs.com and tell me how you are enjoying the book and I will send you the link.

The cure for cancer, as I see it, is rich and complex and not for the faint of heart. It is not a single magic bullet. It involves really rolling up your sleeves and getting to work. You will start on your s/hero's journey to unfolding yourself in all areas of your life, feeling better and better with each step you take.

I do understand the lure of the easy fix, but conventional treatment for cancer is neither easy nor is it a fix. Let's start with Kelly A .Turner's wonderful *Radical Remission: Surviving Cancer Against All Odds.* I strongly recommend you go out right now and buy it. It is one of the three most important books I recommend to people newly diagnosed with cancer. [See Suggested Reading.] In researching people around the world who had experienced spontaneous remission—that is, healing their cancer without Western medical treatment, or sometimes after having been sent home by their doctors who said there is nothing more we can do as in "Go home and 'get your affairs in order'. Turner found they tended to have these nine things in common: They (1) radically changed their diet (2) took control of their health (3) followed their intuition (4) used herbs and supplements (5) released suppressed emotions (6) increased positive emotions (7) embraced social support (8) deepened their spiritual connection (9) had strong reasons for living. Turner's book, too, is rich and complex and will provide you a treasure map for your journey.

[A P.S. My healing story is on Turner's website—radicalremission. com—which got the attention of a student of East London University doing his dissertation on those who chose to heal their cancer naturally, so I became part of a qualitative study on the topic. I had a lengthy Skype interview with London. What fun!]

When I came across her book, I realized my own healing journey reflected her report to the letter, starting with radically changing my diet as you can see in *In Which My Fork Leads the Way*. I took control of my health, making decisions daily to that end. When I could not afford all the possibilites, I let my intuition guide me to select the next best thing. I did use herbs and supplements (see resources online). I saw a therapist to facilitate releasing suppressed emotions (still working on that one) and I increased positive emotions. I reconnected with the world, having pretty much withdrawn from it. Through meditation, Plant Spirit Medicine, qigong, Sacred Fire gatherings (another way of reconnecting with community), I found I could check off all nine points on her list. There is so much we can do to heal! You may not have access to qigong or Plant Spirit Medicine, for example, but you will find your own equivalent. [I do highly recommend them both. See plantspiritmedicine.org for a Plant Spirit Medicine healer near you.]

Let's start the s/hero's journey by celebrating our bodies: let's not see them as broken, but rather as needing loving support to rebalance. Let's love them and see them as not a collection of parts, but as a coherent whole. Let's see our individual lives as part of a whole. Let's ingest as wide a variety of whole foods as we can, be suckled by our beloved Mama Earth and her sun and air and water and plants, her minerals and all that she has to offer. Let's celebrate them daily. Let's breathe them in and hold them sacred.

We are alchemists, all of us. Let's quit playing the victim and step into our power as co-creators of our universe. Let's breathe in our diagnosis, and breathe out marigolds. Let's breathe in the cancer, and breathe out wholeness.

IN PRAISE OF NATUROPATHY
Now, let's look at healing from a slightly different angle, or perhaps really only using a slightly different vocabulary. In the field of naturopathy lie the precepts that surely are the most important

The Vocabulary of Joy

in healing (cancer or anything else) and which are totally and completely abandoned by Western medicine when it comes to the treatment of cancer. I learned the following Naturopathic Principles from the wonderful Naturopathic Doctor Rebecca Word (blueridgenaturopath.com) at whose feet I sat when cancer was new in my life.

> *Primum non nocere* = First, do no harm
> *Vis medicatrix naturae* = Trust in the healing power of nature
> *Tolle causam* = Treat the root cause of disease or imbalance
> *Docere* = Doctor as teacher
> *Tolle totum* = Treat the whole person
> *Praevenire* = Prevention

When considering any form of treatment for my cancer, or for any disease, I first determine if it fits snuggly under these criteria. FOOTNOTE: I remember a phrase from my freshman year in college: something was 'subsumed under the rubric' of something else. I found the phrase equally pretentious and hilarious and it has stuck in my head to this day. So, I make sure that anything I choose for healing must be 'subsumed under the rubric' of these principles. (What a hoot!)

Anyway... if you live in Western North Carolina, I suggest you do whatever you can to include Rebecca Word on your healthcare team. She lives and breathes healing from a *Primum non nocere* perspective.

Speaking of naturopaths, about a decade ago I went to a lovely naturopathic doctor who'd served as in MD when she was in the Air Force. When she left the Air Force, she felt deeply that allopathic medicine did not serve us as well as naturopathic medicine, *so she went back to school and became a naturopathic doctor instead.*

THE ROLE OF INTUITION

When gathering with folks who have chosen to heal their cancer naturally or who are exploring that possibility, one thing some tend to have in common is a feeling of overwhelm when faced with the abundance of things that can be of help. For me, money has been the constraint, not the overabundance of choice, so I have never felt the overwhelm, I just see a glorious abundance of possibilities. But if money is no issue for you, after you have done your research to determine the variety of things that look beneficial to you and your head is still spinning, why not rely on your intuition? What is your 'gut feeling'? They say the gut is actually a second brain (so perhaps that expression has its basis in anatomy). Why not listen to it? I simply ask to be guided to my next best choices. I have not yet mastered using a pendulum or other tools of kinesiology (perhaps one day) so I just, after doing my due diligence, rely on what calls most strongly to me. In fact, I typically don't even have to ask. I just have a 'standing order' to the universe expressing gratitude for guidance and having the welcome mat always at my door.

> *"Not everything that counts can be counted."*
> Denis Burkit, MD

EPIGENETICS, NEUROPLASTICITY, AND PSYCHONEUROIMMUNOLOGY, OH MY!

My doctor introduced me to several new ways of looking at the way we function (I have such rich medical appointments!)

I found online (whatisepigenetics.com) an article called *A Super Brief and Basic Explanation of Epigenetics for Total Beginners* that states: "*Epigenetics Controls Genes. Certain circumstances in life can cause genes to be silenced or expressed over time. In other words, they can be turned off (becoming dormant) or turned on (becoming active). Epigenetics Is Everywhere. What you eat, where you live, who you interact with, when you sleep, how you exercise, even aging – all of these can eventually cause chemical modifications around the genes that will turn those genes on or off over time. Additionally, in certain diseases such as cancer or Alzheimer's, various genes will be switched into the opposite state, away from the normal/healthy state."*

There has been much ado recently about genetics and cancer, witness women who have made the radical choice of having a prophylactic bilateral mastectomy (removing two perfectly healthy breasts) motivated by fear when they learned they had the BRCA genetic mutation. Genetics is not destiny—that is an outdated understanding.

Bruce Harold Lipton is an American developmental biologist best known for promoting the idea that genes and DNA can be manipulated by a person's beliefs. Lipton tells us: *"The Wisdom of Your Cells is a new biology that will profoundly change civilization and the world we live in. This new biology takes us from the belief that we are victims of our genes, that we are biochemical machines, that life is out of our control, into another reality, a reality where our thoughts, beliefs and mind control our genes, our behavior and the life we experience."*

More from Wikipedia: "Psychoneuroimmunology is the study of the interaction between psychological processes and the nervous and immune systems of the human body. Neuroplasticity refers to the potential that the brain has to reorganize by creating new neural pathways to adapt, as it needs. Think of the neurological changes being made in the brain as the brain's way of tuning itself to meet your needs. "

"The new science takes us from victim to creator; we are very powerful in creating and unfolding the lives that we lead. This is actually knowledge of self and if we understand the old axiom, "Knowledge is power," then what we are really beginning to understand is the knowledge of self-power."
Bruce Lipton

HEALING FROM A QIGONG PERSPECTIVE

In a recent qigong class, Brian and Matt taught us something that was a major aHa! for me. It is something called 'push hands' or tuishou (alternately spelled tuei shou or tuei sho.) I checked wikipedia to help me explain it:

"Pushing hands works to undo a person's natural instinct to resist force with force, teaching the body to yield to force and redirect it."

Resisting cancer with the force of chemo and radiation is, well, shall I say "Resistance is futile"?

Tuishou includes:

"ROOTING - Stability of stance, a highly trained sense of balance in the face of force." Yes, cancer prompts us to find our balance, our center, in the face of its force, first and foremost.

"YIELDING - The ability to flow with incoming force from any angle. The practitioner moves with the attacker's force fluidly without compromising their own balance." Yes, we learn to dance with the cancer, dance with the imbalance in our body, to move with the force of the "attack" while maintaining our own balance.

"RELEASE OF POWER (Fa Jing) - The application of power to an opponent. Even while applying force in push hands one maintains the principles of Yielding and Rooting at all times." Yes, in the s/ hero's journey we find our own power and use it wisely and well.

"...Among other things, training with a partner allows a student to develop ting jing (listening power), the sensitivity to feel the direction and strength of a partner's intention"

YES! I find myself, could I say 'developing ting jing'? I am not certain I am using it in just the right context, but in my cancer journey I am finding a greater and greater sensitivity to feeling the

The Vocabulary of Joy

direction and strength of everything, the eb and flow of energy in my body and my environment, in my emotions, in the earth and the sky, in my own heartbeat and the heartbeat of the earth. ('Ting jing' sounds lovely, doesn't it?)

"...qigong aims to treat the whole person, to establish energy balance and spiritual harmony rather than to focus on disease (the realm of medicine). It is healthcare rather than sickcare."

YES. For me, treating the whole person is the *only* valid form of cancer treatment. I know this from qigong, from plant spirit medicine, from my gut, from my readings, from my meditation, from my interactions with others on their s/hero's journey, and from living in Asheville North Carolina where this knowledge is understood on every street corner.

YES YES YES. Matt and Brian, I adore the two of you! As my dear friend Debra Roberts would say, 'I sit at your feet.' Please keep in mind, though, that I am still in qigong kindergarten and Brian and Matt might need to mark up my explanations with a big fat red pen. (Maybe they will contribute to the living book...)

A PEEK AT AYURVEDA
An aside: when I lived in DC, I was blessed to have Nancy Lonsdorf as my doctor, now a bright star in the Ayurveda firmament. That was back in the mid-nineties, and she has aged maybe a week or so. [Like Patrick Hanaway, my doctor at the turn of the century, is a bright star in the Functional Medicine firmament. Perhaps Brian Lewis will be a bright star in a firmament of his own...]

"...cancer is a complex, multifactorial, and heterogenous disease which requires innovative approaches in translational and personalized medicine."
Cancer, Inflammation, and Insights from Ayurveda
Venil N. Sumantran 1 ,* and Girish Tillu 2

"In this context, we discuss the ayurvedic concept of "Ama" which is thought to be a toxic, proinflammatory waste-product of improper digestion. We then develop hypotheses and outline preclinical and clinical experiments designed to prove whether 'Ama' can serve as a novel and reliable biomarker that links abnormal digestive status, with the onset of chronic inflammation. Although personalized medicine is new to modern medicine, it is well established in Ayurveda, the traditional system of Indian medicine which is still being practiced."

Ayurveda, like Traditional Chinese Medicine, like naturopathy, like I expect all traditional healing, is about establishing balance. They are all about seeing the body as a living system and not a collection of independent parts in one human envelope. They are all about building health, not about killing the Big Bad Boogeyman cancer.

I propose that the epidemic of cancer and our appalling lack of ability to deal with it serves a similar purpose for Western medicine as an individual's dance with cancer. Cancer is not so much a physical illness as it is a wake-up call for us all as a community, as society, to recognize that the whole universe conspires to bring us healing. The natural world offers healing in abundance. In the 'living book', I will share with you what I call The Asheville Protocol – the list of things I am doing or would like to do if I could afford them. Remember I have no authority or expertise beyond my own intuition and a lot of reading and talking with other folks on the path of healing cancer naturally.

SWIMMING IN SILENCE

> *"I think 99 times and find nothing. I stop thinking, swim in silence, and the truth comes to me."*
> Albert Einstein

The Vocabulary of Joy

In Which I Find the Cure for Cancer

*"All profound things and emotions of things are
preceded and attended by silence."*
Herman Melville

*"Silence vibrating is Creation. Silence flowing is Love. Silence
shared is Friendship. Silence seen is Infinity. Silence heard is
Adoration. Silence expressed is Beauty. Silence maintained is
Strength. Silence omitted is Suffering. Silence allowed is Rest.
Silence recorded is Scripture. Silence preserved is Our Tradition.
Silence given is Initiating. Silence received is Joy. Silence perceived
is Knowledge. Silence stabilized is Fulfillment. Silence alone is."*
Maharishi Mahesh Yogi

I came across and article the other day on lifehack.org that said:
*Science Says Silence Is Much More Important To Our Brains Than
We Think.* The article went on to say, *"The scientists discovered
that when the mice were exposed to two hours of silence per day
they developed new cells in the hippocampus. The hippocampus
is a region of the brain associated with memory, emotion and
learning."* I got to thinking (and googling) about silence and
healing. The concept is not at all new to me because I do...

TM IN THE AM AND THE PM
I have a firm basis for nourishing mind/body/spirit: I have been
practicing Transcendental Meditation™ since 1972. That practice
has kept me humming steadily ever since. TM is a simple, natural
technique that produces a profoundly deep state of restful
alertness. It allows the mind to 'transcend' the normal waking state
of consciousness and reach a state of pure consciousness that
has been carefully documented for the last forty some years. The
Mayo Clinic says: "Transcendental meditation is a simple, natural
technique... This form of meditation allows your body to settle into
a state of profound rest and relaxation and your mind to achieve
a state of inner peace, without needing to use concentration or
effort." The Cleveland Clinic says: "Transcendental Meditation
doesn't focus on breathing or chanting, like other forms of

meditation. Instead, it encourages a restful state of mind beyond thinking... A 2009 study found Transcendental Meditation helped alleviate stress in college students, while another found it helped reduce blood pressure, anxiety, depression and anger." and Forbes magazine says: "Perhaps its greatest benefit is that it's relatively quick to learn and easy to master. No waiting weeks or months of practice before you see results: TM cuts right to the chase, taking only days — or for some, minutes — before one feels reprieve from their painful and overwhelming thoughts." And if you are looking for "evidence-based" meditation, I doubt any other form of meditation has been so thoroughly studied (or has been practiced for millenia). Herbert Benson is widely credited with naming "the relaxation response" but his introduction to what he named the relaxation response was actually from research on TM, way back in the day.

IT TAKES A VILLAGE

"In my village, houses do not have doors that can be locked. They have entrances. The absence of doors is not a sign of technological deprivation but an indication of the state of mind the community is in. The open door symbolizes the open mind and open heart. Thus a doorless home is home to anybody in the community."
Malidoma Some

While I loved living way out in the country, it was also very lonely. Now I live in a beautiful 14-story, classic, almost 100 year old building with plenty of people around and a good friend right next door. In fact, when this was a hotel long ago, a door used to connect our two apartments. We have joked about uncovering the old door and putting it to good use. I love the sense that this building is a village. In fact, I often leave my front door wide open, not only to have a lovely breeze from the window down the hall, but also as Malidoma Some says above, to create a "doorless home" to welcome anybody in the community.

In Which I Find the Cure for Cancer

In the other sense of "village", I have received all kinds of healing from all kinds of people. The highlights: In my healing journey I have seen my beloved OT Diane Douglas who does Integrative Manual Therapy which is the most fabulous bodywork imaginable, Lara Ferguson Diaz for her wonderful acupuncture, energy workers, a tiny bit of massage (I'd love much more), a brief foray with a belly dancing class, a chiropractor, a therapist, naturopath Rebecca Word, Marianne Mitchell (Shamanic Energy Medicine, Ageless Wisdom teacher, Spiritual Counselor, Modern Day Priestess!) and best of all, Lisa Lichtig, my Plant Spirit Medicine Healer. Again and again, my instincts guide me to what I need to heal.

"All our progress is an unfolding, like the vegetable bud, you have first an instinct, then an opinion, then a knowledge, as the plant has root, bud, and fruit. Trust the instinct to the end, though you can render no reason."
~ Ralph Waldo Emerson

PRAYER

Prayer has been used in service of healing probably in all cultures, in all times. Larry Dossey's 1996 book *Prayer Is Good Medicine: How to Reap the Healing Benefits of Prayer* and his 1995 book *Healing Words: The Power of Prayer and the Practice of Medicine* are modern day reminders of that. Amazon says of his work: *"Proving prayer to be as valid and vital a healing tool as drugs or surgery, the bestselling author of Meaning & Medicine and Recovering the Soul offers a bold integration of science and spirituality."* What may have been bold in the mid nineties is more of a "Yes, of course!" today.

A prayer that speaks deeply to me and says what I want to say about healing is "A Call to Prayer" from The United Nations Environmental Sabbath Service:

We who have lost our sense and our senses – our touch, our smell, our vision of who we are; we who frantically force and press all things, without rest for body or spirit, hurting our earth and injuring ourselves: we call a halt.

We want to rest. We need to rest and allow the earth to rest. We need to reflect and to rediscover the mystery that lives in us, that is the ground of every unique expression of life, the source of the fascination that calls all things to communion. We declare a Sabbath, a space of quiet: for simple being and letting be; for recovering the great, forgotten truths; for learning how to live again.

OUR OWN HANDS
I am drawn to learn more about using water, sound, light, color, music, and essential oils for healing. Frankincense and myrrh have been shown to be powerful tools in healing cancer. No wonder they were chosen as gifts fit for a king! And then there is energy work of all kinds: my training is in Reiki and Reconnective Healing.

If I went into detail on all the types of healing nature provides, it would take volumes to hold it all.

STILL OVERWHELMED?
I have included in this chapter a small subset of tools for healing. I invite you, instead of feeling overwhelmed, to revel in the abundance of nature's healing gifts. Even revel in the abundance of words that mean abundance! There's profusion, plentifulness, profuseness, copiousness, amplitude, lavishness, bountifulness, bounty. Revel in the words that mean revel: enjoy, delight in, love, like, adore, be pleased by, take pleasure in, appreciate, relish, lap up, savor, get a kick out of. Does Earth offer too many kinds of trees? Too many kinds of flowers? Too many kinds of squashes? Don't let abundance, profusion, plentifulness, profuseness, copiousness, amplitude, lavishness, bountifulness, bounty throw you! Follow your heart, follow your guidance, follow your dreams. Abandon the search for the magic bullet. Healing is everywhere.

The Vocabulary of Joy

In Which I Step Into My Power

"In the depths of winter I finally learned that
within me there lay an invincible summer."
Albert Camus

As I sit here I am looking at a cut on my wrist, not quite an inch long. It is pink still and possibly a wee bit warm. It is visible evidence of my body healing itself. The flesh was torn on something, I don't quite remember what, but it is healing. My body knows how to heal. What a lovely, reassuring sight!

Inside my body, my belly is healing, my kidney-space is healing. All is well. Maybe something else will slip out of balance in the future, but my body and I can handle it. My spirit is healing. I had my own Dark Night of the Soul some years ago, and I walked through it and came out the other side. And I have it on good authority that one day I will die/pass/croak, and that is good too.

But in the meantime, I have learned (am learning) how to connect with my breath and my qi and my somewhat-messed-up-but-that's-okay body. I have learned to find healing everywhere. I have learned how to seek and find balance and harmony, and when it slips away, find it again. Everything, everywhere is supporting me.

Celebrating the Blessings of Life with Cancer

Julie Savage Parker

"She made broken look beautiful
and strong look invincible.
She walked with the Universe
on her shoulders and made it
look like a pair of wings."
Ariana Dancu

I sit here at 9:19 on a Thursday morning and the clouds outside my window I think are putting on a show just for me. The air smells sweet and a flock of birds is swooping and circling with great joy outside my 9th floor window. (I wonder how they know I am on the 9th floor?)

Cancer has taught me to see healing everywhere. It has taught me to make better decisions every day. Now the truth is, I may eat Cheetos again one day, but I can correct and re-correct my course. I can make and re-make my story. My flesh will be torn again, and it will heal again. I feel broken and remade, held in 'warm sunskin hands' and made whole with all that is. The poetry of Alla Renée Bozarth touched me deeply before my cancer journey began and helped carry me safely through it. With her kind permission, I include it here that it may help guide you in your own journey of healing.

Bakerwoman God

Bakerwoman God, I am your living bread.
Strong, brown Bakerwoman God,
I am your low, soft and being-shaped loaf.

I am your rising bread,
well-kneaded by some divine
and knotty pair of knuckles,
by your warm earth hands.
I am bread well-kneaded.

The Vocabulary of Joy

In Which I Step Into My Power

Put me in fire, Bakerwoman God,
put me in your own bright fire.
I am warm, warm as you from fire.
I am white and gold, soft and hard,
brown and round. I am so warm from fire.

Break me, Bakerwoman God.
I am broken under your caring Word.
Drop me in your special juice in pieces.
Drop me in your blood.
Drunken me in the great red flood.
Self-giving chalice, swallow me.
My skin shines in the divine wine.
My face is cup-covered and I drown.

I fall up, in a red pool in a gold world
where your warm sunskin hand is there
to catch and hold me.
Bakerwoman God, remake me.

Alla Renée Bozarth

Womanpriest: A Personal Odyssey 1978, 1988, distributed by Alla
Renée Bozarth; Moving to the Edge of the World, iUniverse 2000;
and This is My Body~ Praying for Earth, Prayers from the Heart,
iUniverse 2004. Find "Bakerwoman God" available as graphic art
card or in frameable wall plaque size here: bearblessings.com

SUGGESTED READING

If you buy nothing else, get these first three books. In fact, the first two should be in everyone's library, cancer or not!

Crazy Sexy Diet
by Kris Carr [kriscarr.com]

Mind Over Medicine
by Lissa Rankin, MD [lissarankin.com]

Radical Remission ~ Surviving Cancer Against All Odds
by Kelly A. Turner, PhD [radicalremission.com]

The Biology of Belief
by Bruce Harold Lipton, PhD [brucelipton.com]

Close to the Bone ~ Life-Threatening Illness as a Soul Journey
by Jean Shinoda Bolen, MD

Traditional Chinese Medicine Approches to Cancer: Harmony in the Face of the Tiger
by Henry McGrath

You Are the Placebo: Making Your Mind Matter
by Dr. Joe Dispenza

Journey of Souls: Case Studies of Life Between Lives
by Michael Newton

Destiny of Souls: New Case Studies of Life Between Lives
by Michael Newton

Dying to Be Me
by Anita Moorjani

The Cancer-Fighting Kitchen, Second Edition: Nourishing, Big-Flavor Recipes for Cancer Treatment and Recovery
by Rebecca Katz and Mat Edelson

The Longevity Kitchen: Satisfying, Big-Flavor Recipes Featuring the Top 16 Age-Busting Power Foods [120 Recipes for Vitality and Optimal Health
by Rebecca Katz and Mat Edelson

The Slow Down Diet ~ Eating for Pleasure, Energy, & Weight Loss
by Marc David [psychologyofeating.com]

WEBSITES

chrisbeatcancer.com
thetruthaboutcancer.com
healingcancernaturally.com
julieparker.me
plantspiritmedicine.com
drhyman.com
michaelpollan.com
wendellberrybooks.com
tm.org

The Vocabulary of Joy

WRITING FOR HEALING

"We do not write in order to be understood;
we write in order to understand."
C. Day-Lewis

"In times of trouble, Mother Mary comes to me, speaking words of wisdom", write it out, write it out...

Writing for me has been an exceedingly powerful tool for healing. At the turn of the century, I walked through a big, mean, ugly, Dark Night of the Soul. Writing got me through it! In this segment of *The Vocabulary of Joy*, I include excerpts from my blog julieparker. me and three pieces I wrote at that time that helped me express, then understand, and eventually move beyond what I was experiencing. They are *Julie Dumpty*, *Planting Groundhogs*, and *I Lost My Mother in the Backseat of My Car*, part of my book (as yet unpublished) called *Planting Groundhogs: Essays on the Evolution of a Woman's Soul*.

In my current cancer journey, I started my blog (at julieparker.me) the day after I got out of the hospital, and two years ago I decided to write this book. The book has helped me sort out the whole mishmash of the journey and the road ahead.

I have never understood some of the major writers of our time who complain about the act of writing. Dorothy Parker famously quipped: "I hate writing, I love having written." For me, writing has always been easy and joyful and it has helped me listen to my own mind/body rhythms—I can always tell when I am about to give birth to some words and I run to the computer and let them loose.

I have also included in the Writing for Healing segment *Yet Another Julie*—writing I found on Facebook by a cancer compadre who is using Facebook extensively to write her heart out in her very intensive and painful cancer journey. She graciously gave me permission to include it in the book.

julieparker.me

"Your body is amazing. No matter what you are doing now or what you have done in the past, your body is constantly working to balance and heal."

Paula Powell

My blog (at julieparker.me) gives a picture of what I was feeling when I was in the thick of it, as opposed to now, three years later. Below are some sample posts from the blog, starting with *Yesterday*, the very first post. Whitman and I decided to leave it as is, meaning there might be a typo or two. Forgive us.

Yesterday
October 10. 2013

Yesterday my friend JN picked me up at Mission Hospital after my week-long stay following surgery to remove all my "lady bits": abdominal hysterectomy, oophorectomy (isn't that a delightful word?), and a third label I can't remember at the moment. On the way home, I was about a minus 17 on the life force index… totally worn out. Most of JN's questions I could not answer: "I don't know." and "I don't know." and "I don't know." and eventually "I don't know and I don't care."

Celebrating the Blessings of Life with Cancer   139

But this is not really a blog about cancer. It is instead a story of
the wonders that have started unfolding in the last two weeks
of dancing with cancer. Synchronicities, blessings, and magic.
Yesterday was the only low day, really. I feel terrific today. But I am
getting ahead of myself – I will go back to September 24th, the day
this all started.

It comes to a head
OCTOBER 10, 2013

By Tuesday September 24th, I had not really eaten a meal for a
couple of months – maybe 1/2 sandwich a day, if that. One day I
only had one cup of ginger tea. That Tuesday I called my doctor's
office and said that I still had no appetite and my stomach was
quite bloated. I was told to get in immediately, and while my
own doctor (BL) was completely booked, they set me up with his
partner, (CK). They drew blood, Dr. CK poked me in the belly, my
own doctor stuck his head in to poke a few extra times, and then
they decided to send me for a CT scan lickety split. The very next
day I was full of 'contrast' (a concoction actually based on Country
Time Lemonade) sliding through the CT scan, and the results
followed the next day, Wednesday.

Wednesday afternoon I found a phone message from Dr. BL that
said GET TO THE EMERGENCY ROOM NOW – three times in one
message. So my friend DD (more about her later) and her honey
drove me to the emergency room. We arrived at 9, they drew
blood, and then wanted to do a urinalysis. I couldn't pee. 10pm,
still no pee. 11pm, still no pee. They gave me 3 LARGE cups of
water, and still no pee. They started talking catheter, which terrified
me. By 2:30 am, I was so concerned about DD and her honey, still
stuck in the ER waiting for me. I finally gave in to the catheter, and
that was the first in a series of things about which I had concern
and they turned out to be no biggie. This is the first MAIN POINT
of the whole blog – that fears so often are groundless – that we
create our own panic. *"There is nothing either good or bad but
thinking makes it so."* Hamlet

The Vocabulary of Joy

The following Thursday

As I was lying by myself for hours in pre-op, I decided to paint my own canvas regarding this whole thing. "What can I do to make this a fun experience?" I asked myself. All the folks in surrounding cubicles seemed to have someone with them, so there were lots of tender conversations going on all around me. I loved that gentle murmur, and I loved listening to other languages (I picked out Spanish and something unidentifiable) and that was fun. The journey had begun, and I was steering the ship.

The second MAIN POINT is what I have decided to call a PAH! Moment. A bit of background: when I lived in DC I got very involved with the Deaf community and Deaf culture. (I got my MS at Gallaudet University in DC where all undergrads are deaf.) I learned at the knee of a fabulous ASL (American Sign Language) poet Clayton Valli the extent of the sign PAH! Meaning success, or, at last. My days in the hospital were full of blessings large and small, each one a little explosion of joy. That reminded me of "PAH!" – an unexpected moment of joy. [I am taking liberties just a bit with the meaning of PAH.] As I started noticing and appreciating more and more of them, more and more lined up at the door waiting to come into my experience.

One thing that I have loved LOVED is so much touch – from doctors, nurses, and CNAs. The pain of living without human touch has worked up to a fever pitch in the last few months. Odd that I chose to address it by manifesting cancer and a week in the hospital. I am probably one of very few people who actually loved being in the hospital – all of that human contact. I even loved when they came into my room in the middle of the night!

SOME OF MY PAH! MOMENTS:

NO PAIN – ALL GAIN. I have had no pain following surgery. What a blessing, eh? They had me on IV pain meds directly afterwards and perhaps my body would have felt pain then, but everyone

Celebrating the Blessings of Life with Cancer

– doctors, nurses, CNAs (certified nurse assistants), friends – everyone expected there to be pain. Pain had not even come across my radar screen before everyone was asking about it – I had been neither expecting it nor dreading it. I have turned down oxycodone, percocet, even extra strength tylenol, as none of it was necessary. PAH!

THE LANGUAGE of FLOWERS
I really wanted something to read. I know years ago, volunteers would push around a cart with books and magazines for folks to read. I was told that does not happen anymore. But my friend DST sent me an email through Mission's website, but they told her it would not go through on the weekend. Well, Sat. morning a volunteer delivered her email to my room (what a treat!) I was chatting with the volunteer talking about yearning for something to read and he said, "Well let me see." and he came back in MINUTES with a lovely book *The Language of Flowers* he had borrowed from the nurse's station. PAH!

Mission Hospital has [had] a wonderful integrative health program. Essential oils have made a huge difference in my life and to have them in the hospital is SO healing! And I had a lovely hand and foot massage. Alas, the dogs were only there on Fridays – I SO WOULD HAVE LOVED THAT. But anyway, PAH!

My Kingdom for a piece of toast. After days of nothing but clear broth and then only a choice of cream of chicken soup or (hospital) mashed potatoes, I started craving toast, and toast appeared with my very next meal. Next I craved toast with jelly, and that came with my very next meal. Heaven. PAH!

My cousin Jim steps into the picture. I had three good friends as my health care power of attorneys when my cousin Jim who went to appointments with their family friend Judith for 10 years (she had ovarian cancer) volunteered to step in. He is a very sharp guy and now has 10 years experience with ovarian cancer as well as with the

The Vocabulary of Joy

system. He is working on seeing if he can get me on Medicaid. PAH!

A nurse named Cyndie came in with a lovely little crocheted throw her mother makes for patients for me to keep. PAH!

Lovenox helps prevent blood clots after major surgery. They come as shots that I have to give myself in the stomach daily for 2 weeks. I dreaded them so, but turns out they are easy peasy. PAH!

Death, Dying, and the Midnight Willies
OCTOBER 12, 2013
I have never been afraid of death, but that dying stuff is another story. One night in the wee hours, I got to contemplating my actual death. One of the wonderful CNAs was in my room checking my vitals and I asked her to be straight with me about dying and what actually happens for women with cancer. She very kindly sat with me for over an hour while we talked turkey. I am not at death's door – not even at death's driveway, but I have never before even been on the same block, and have questions. I am not afraid of the answers.

Longing for a Rebounder
OCTOBER 13, 2013
Something has been telling me the past couple of years to get a rebounder (a mini-trampoline). Now that I am dancing with cancer, I see why. I know that exercise is really important when healing from cancer and using a rebounder is about the best exercise around and NEEDAK is the best made, safest. I am going to put it out to the Universe to manifest one. I bet it will happen as easily as the toast!
[UPDATE: It came! A friend called me about a week later and told me she had a Needak in her car and she was headed my way!]

Oxytocin vs Oxycodone
OCTOBER 14, 2013
Oxycodone is the pain-numbing narcotic that folks get into trouble with. Oxytocin is the stuff of bliss that comes from human touch.

Celebrating the Blessings of Life with Cancer   143

(See In Praise Of Casual Intimacy *that I wrote more than a decade ago.) I can envision a whole new area of medicine that is just about smiling and touch. My gynecologic oncologist surgeon (that is a mouthful, eh?) is Dr Ashley Case – a wonderful warm woman with a team of folks working with her who are all so very dear and they seem to know about the value of touch. I have had almost no human touch for decades and I am convinced of its healing power. One night in the hospital when I was dancing with the midnight willies, one of my favorite nurses came in and I asked her to hold my hand. I turned down the oxycodone they offered, but I am willing to beg for the oxytocin.*

Bragging Rights
OCTOBER 15, 2013

I forgot to say – my main tumor was the proverbial football size… one of my poor ovaries was carrying that around for some time. AND they removed 3 and a half LITERS of fluid from my belly. Can you imagine? What a way to lose weight, huh? They said they took out 8 pounds of stuff, not counting the fluid. Yech…

Prognosis
OCTOBER 16, 2013

Prognosis – a glass half full, glass half empty sort of a word. When teetering on the edge of fear, it can be chilling. When filled with a mix of optimism and joy, it can be a springboard to a glowing future. They want me to do another CT scan on Friday… to check out the pancreas and surrounding neighborhood. Right now I am dancing with one toe in optimism and one in fear.

How many dogs?
OCTOBER 17, 2013

How many dogs do I have time for? I measure the length of my life in dogs… Right now I have my dear 15 year old Anna. I moved to Asheville in 1997 with my beloved Cricket and added dear dear Charley and sweet Freya in 2002.

The Vocabulary of Joy

Am I going to have time for any more dogs? If I go sooner rather than later, that is the one thing I would really miss. Could I please have one more dog, Universe, or one more set of 2 or 3? . . . Or is there no more time for dogs?

To Live or Not to Live …
That is the Question
OCTOBER 21, 2013

I have procrastinated writing about my Friday appointment. After applying plenty of pressure to my oncologist, she finally said I have "months to years" to live. She said she really wanted to wait until after my CT scan to make a prediction. Turns out I could not take the CT scan (one blood measurement was too high and another too low) so they will schedule me for an MRI this week. I am rolling the "months" prognosis around in my mouth a bit before I spit it out.

Waiting on the MRI
OCTOBER 25, 2013

I am thinking of all the folks waiting on tests. I had my MRI yesterday to look for a second cancer – half an hour in a tube about two inches from my nose. I just closed my eyes and couldn't see how scary it was – or maybe just how claustrophobic.

Now I am waiting on the results which they said they would have yesterday. And waiting, and waiting. I am holding the phone in my lap and even taking it to the bathroom with me. I hope they don't make me wait over the weekend. Perhaps I should close my eyes?

I love my guts!
OCTOBER 25, 2013

All pink and shiny and cancer-free, so says yesterday's MRI.

Oh Lordy – the dang mirror!
OCTOBER 29, 2013

I just looked in the mirror – and was horrified! I look absolutely

Celebrating the Blessings of Life with Cancer

awful. Small children will shriek and cling to their mamas. The extreme (and sudden) weight loss + leftover effects of anesthesia and other medicine + stress + exhaustion +, +, +. I had been excited about being seen (for the weight loss) but now I prefer to become a hermit.

I have quit eating apples...
OCTOBER 31, 2013
...because I DO NOT WANT to keep the doctor away! My doctor (BL) is so insightful, on so many levels. Tuesday I had my first follow-up appointment with him following my cancer surgery. Two close friends (DR and JN who both serve as my healthcare power of attorney) came along. JN was blown away by him, by his insight and the breadth of his approach. DR is a friend of his and was the person who sent me his way to begin with.

BL talked about my body undergoing so many changes at the moment (surgery and major weight loss) and my body parts having to reposition themselves vis à vis other body parts – a perfect metaphor for my whole life now. Everything in my life is changing and I am crying out for what DR calls my 'Sacred Next'. Dr. BL has my number, and he is nudging me forward (along with DR and JN) to my Sacred Next. (Not the Big Sacred Next, because that is still years off, we are envisioning.)

[For those of you who do not know me or have not seen me recently, know that I have been using a walker for the last year or so – a balance issue caused by my brain bleeding. A bit of knowledge you need for this next paragraph.]

Anyway, when I got home on Tuesday and got out of the car to open the gate, I stepped forward where I could no longer hold onto the car but not near enough to the gate to grab it. I just stood and teetered there for maybe five minutes – afraid to go forward and afraid to walk backwards. Metaphor galore. (I finally got the nerve to walk forward, teetering and crouching, but I reached the

The Vocabulary of Joy

gate, and opened it.) And something about the four of us in that room – each I think with a Key to my new life. But I am still nearer the car than the gate.

47 Years Ago...
NOVEMBER 6, 2013

...I was the assistant editor of my high school literary magazine. They asked me to write the dedication and here it is:

> *The young people of my generation write of death, or unrequited love, of man's inhumanity to man. It is well to acknowledge the ills of our world, but to play Don Quixote and to charge at every foreboding windmill on the landscape is worse than foolish. Let us learn a little more of life before we condemn it. Let us only destroy as we are prepared to rebuild. Let us search out the beauty, and the goodness, and the love in our lives, for they are always there.*

This was my intent when we started WNC WOMAN. I so hope to have another platform to speak of this before I hand in my dinner pail.

Blown Back
JANUARY 1, 2014

I allowed myself to be blown away yesterday when my primary care doc (who I am pretty sure walks on water) suggested I at least consider 'poisoning' myself with chemotherapy. When I saw this quotation this morning on Facebook, I was blown back.

"Drugs never cure disease. They merely hush the voice of nature's protest, and pull down the danger signals she erects along the pathway of transgression. Any poison taken into the system has to be reckoned with later on even though it palliates present symptoms. Pain may disappear, but the patient is left in a worse condition, though unconscious of it at the time." Daniel. H. Kress, M.D.

Celebrating the Blessings of Life with Cancer   147

Full of Myself
JANUARY 2, 2014

I have been full of myself since cancer appeared on the scene. I
was so proud of the fact that I decided to heal naturally with
nutrition, meditation, rebounding, etc. I was judgmental of folks
who mindlessly chose the slash/burn/poison route. I am still
very comfortable with my choice. For me, I so resonate with the
natural route that it was never actually a decision, which implies
slash/burn/poison was ever in the running; it was more "Oh, of
course this is what I will do!" But as I looked around at sites like
ihadcancer and similar ones where folks going through it can
connect, I realized how very fortunate I am to be 64 and have
ovarian cancer. I don't need anything they removed. Never did,
actually. I still have my lungs and my colon and my pancreas and all
the bits you need for daily living, and they all seem to be in good
working order. What a good thing! I never felt pain and I feel
terrific now. The cancer is barely a blip on my radar screen.

Who am I writing this for?
JANUARY 3, 2014

I got the idea to do a blog while I was still in the hospital,
longing for a laptop so I could get it 'on paper' while it was still
fresh. Friends were checking in so regularly I thought it would be
a good way to keep everyone informed at once. When I realized
I was surrounded by blessing after blessing in the hospital, it
occurred to me that being showered by blessings while still in
the hospital after major surgery might not be the most common
experience, and I really wanted to shout it out. Being terrified of
cancer doesn't – wait, let me re-phrase that. LETTING GO of the
terror can help heal from cancer. I have chosen to make cancer
my friend, to welcome its gifts, thus encouraging it to say ,"Well,
my job here is done," and take off.
I sometimes wish ONLY strangers were reading this. Then I
could really be TOTALLY open. Now I am not so sure how much

The Vocabulary of Joy

I am holding back. The blog is excellent therapy for me and some friends pitch in with their reactions. A dear friend, a very treasured friend (DR), emailed me this morning in response to my last post "FULL OF MYSELF" and asked "Who better to be full of?" I laughed but then realized that I am claiming myself in the process of healing. I am claiming my power and my authority and my internal wisdom. "Yaho yahey!" as DR would say. I am indeed full of mySelf and proud of it!

Solar Cycle 24
JANUARY 7, 2014

They say the sun has flipped upside down while reversing magnetic poles. Really. This happened very recently, during Solar Cycle 24, and it is a Really Big Deal. See NASA's website.

I figured something really big happened, because on Sunday I found myself with a scarf wrapped low on my hips, belly dancing!! No, I am not kidding. And I loved it! Mind you I am pretty inept at the moment and not even sure if I will ever be 'ept', but it was great fun and so unlike me. Or perhaps exactly like the new me, my 'new normal'. The belly dancing class put on by the wonderful new non-profit (or soon to finish the 501(c)3 process) Journey to be Free Naturally. I actually wrote an article about it on the stands now: *The Answer to Cancer?* So I guess you will find me every Sunday at 5:30 working on moving various body parts (while holding other body parts still.) Tricky. I think I will start with snake arms…

Lots of 'new normals' on the scene and all great fun. Well, all positive, anyway. As I sit here I am in minute 14 of 'oil pulling'. Ever heard of it? I only stumbled on the idea in the last few months and this morning is my first day of trying it. …. Okay it is later and I have done it. I put a glob of coconut oil in my mouth and swished it around for 20 minutes. It was not bad at all and now afterwards I feel my body thanking me. You are supposed to do it first thing in the morning, then spit it out outside or in the trash or something as it is chock full of toxins. Click on the link oil pulling to read more about it. Next habit to develop is the neti pot. Yes, I do believe the sun must have flipped upside down!

I'm Having a Love Affair
JANUARY 30, 2014

… with my body! I had broccoli and spinach for breakfast. After my morning lemon water, of course. My little fridge is full of healthy stuff, and I am actually eating it rather than turning into a science experiment. My integrative medicine doctor could poke his nose in for a pop inspection, and I would pass with flying colors. The last time I wanted to slather mayonnaise on a sandwich, I decided I didn't really want it. (And I am now using a very healthy organic mayo.)

I decided to focus on the good stuff I wanted to add to my diet, not the bad stuff I wanted to take away. And that is working for me! I am putting turmeric in just about everything, as that is a Big Time anti-cancer agent. I even sprinkle it on my ice cream…. (Just kidding. No ice cream, no sugar.)
And I love love love roasted cauliflower. I have fresh parsley and fresh cilantro in the fridge ready to add to a green smoothie or a meal.
I finally don't miss meat. I am not a vegetarian (yet?) but I am happy with a veggie meal.

Now about an ACTUAL love affair…

!SPLAT!
FEBRUARY 1, 2014

Thursday was the first day of my *LiveStrong at the Y* program for folks with cancer. Well, it was actually the day my group got tested for upper and lower body strength, reach, how-long-we-can-stand-on-one-foot, and the testing started with how many laps we could walk in 6 minutes, checking our pulse at the beginning and at the end. I volunteered to be in the first group… we went four at a time. 3 minutes into it, I went splat! on the floor. Hard. They stopped the whole test and came running over to check on me. They insisted I stay down for a bit. I determined that nothing was broken, and nothing really even bent. I do have a bump on my arm, but otherwise unbruised, unembarrassed... and unfazed. Falls are funny things though, aren't they? I wish I had it on tape so I could get a better idea what actually happened. I was trying to keep up with the other folks in the group and I guess my four-wheeled walker got away from me. Not sure if I got dizzy – it all happened so fast.

Anyway, I am taking a tai chi class tomorrow (or taijiquan is the spelling they use) put on by Integrative Family Medicine of Asheville. I may fall flat on my face like I did at the Y, but I am going to do it anyway. So there.

Food as 'Chemotherapy'
FEBRUARY 25, 2014
"Let food be thy medicine and medicine be thy food" Hippocrates

NO WAY, JOSÉ
I put my foot down, crossed my arms, and shook my head. "No! No chemotherapy. No way. I refuse to abuse my body in that way. I will not go the slash/burn/poison route!" (Or did I say "What are you, nuts? Get away from me with that [stuff]!" (insert a less polite word of your choice))

SO, WHAT?
But what, then? Ovarian cancer took up residence in my body this fall. It may be gone now... or it may not be. Okay, I did the 'slash' part of the deal—they removed about everything but my tonsils (including my appendix) but chemotherapy is where I draw the line.

WHAT NOTS
"Well, Julie," I told myself. "If you refuse to poison your body to get well, (what a concept!) you will just have to nurture your body and

Celebrating the Blessings of Life with Cancer

see if that does the trick!" and that is what I have done. In effect, I took my own 'Hippocratic oath' and let food be my medicine. And instead of focusing on what I was omitting (sugar—esp. the demon high fructose corn syrup, wheat, processed food, fast food, gluten, most dairy, etc.) I focused on savoring the most nutritious foods I could get my hands on. I have finally gone all organic when at all possible. I learned that the following foods are critical to buy organic: apples, celery, cherry tomatoes, cucumber, grapes, hot peppers, nectarines, peaches, potatoes, spinach, strawberries, sweet bell peppers, collards & kale, summer squash & zucchini.

KALE, KALE, THE GANG'S ALL HERE

And speaking of kale—eat it! Develop a taste for it if you have to, but eat it even if you have to hold your nose at first. I eventually found it to be yummy. I bet you will too, if you are not already a fan. It is my least favorite leafy green, I admit—I much prefer chard and spinach. But kale is a powerhouse of nutrition so I was determined to learn to love it. (Love, not fear, you know, is the name of the game.) Don't fear kale. Don't fear vegetables at all! Honor them. Savor them. And thank the farmers who lovingly tended them without chemical pesticides and with honor for Mother Earth.

I have been strongly influenced by Ayurveda… [from altmedicine. about.com: Ayurveda, also known as Ayurvedic Medicine, is the traditional medicine of India, which originated there over 5,000 years ago. Ayurveda emphasizes re-establishing balance in the body through diet, lifestyle, exercise, and body cleansing, and the health of the mind, body, and spirit.] A typical day for me starts with a glass of lemon water, and then a stewed apple with cinnamon, and whatever else I am inspired to add. Organic, of course, and fresh. Ayurveda believes that you need to eat lightly in the morning… and that the 'digestive fire' peaks at noon so lunch should be your main meal. There is a wonderful Ayurvedic recipe to get the digestive fire stirred up before a meal: grated carrots, chopped fresh parsley, a few squeezes of lemon juice and a bit of

The Vocabulary of Joy

freshly grated ginger.

And later in the day, sometimes I eat kitcheree (kitchade/kidgeree/kitcheri/kichdi—it has a thousand more spellings). Kitcheree is basmati rice with mung/moong dal (spell these any way you like too). [Thanks, Dr. L, for introducing me to this stuff!] Ideally you soak the rice and the dal the night before. Kitcheree is a classic and famed for its healing properties, being very soothing and easy to digest. It is typically the first solid food given to babies. It is great with fresh cilantro on top. Google it for some ideas. FYI: Ayurveda insists that cold things, like ice water, douse the digestive fire and are a big no-no. I like a nice hot cup of Holy Basil(tulsi) tea. [Another thanks to Dr. L.]

VEGGIN' OUT
These days I find myself actually daydreaming of broccoli. (Okay, sometimes I still daydream of molten lava cake with ice cream and a cherry on top, but broccoli more and more is winning out.) Broccoli sprouts. Rinsing my first batch now.

Veggie smoothies—ahhh. Got myself a Vitamix (vitamix.com) and am going to town. Fresh baby spinach in everything. NO ICE! And either some fresh ginger or lemon (or both?). English cucumbers. Celery. And whatever alkaline veggie floats your boat.

For cancer, I throw garlic and ginger and turmeric into just about everything… and to activate the turmeric, black pepper and a fat of some kind (olive oil or ghee, typically). For general health, I have started putting freshly ground flax seeds and chia seeds on just about everything too.

EATING ALKALINE
A few years ago, my friend Nina introduced me to the work of Dr. Robert Young who writes of the importance of eating 80% alkaline foods. Really important. Really, really important. Look up his site. If you follow his suggestions, you will thank me. More and more I

Celebrating the Blessings of Life with Cancer

am reading about the importance of eating alkaline. Yes, the body maintains a constant ph all by itself, but if your diet is too acid, the body makes some ugly trade-offs to do so. (See phmiracleliving. com)

TO [X] OR NOT TO [X]

I can't say that I have made a final decision on meat. Organic, humanely raised and honored, yes, for now. Even the milk I buy is from cows whose tails have not been docked. (I didn't even realize there was such a thing as tail docking until I saw it on the carton.) But I am also more and more picking up almond or coconut milk. Dairy or not to dairy, that is the question. Mushrooms or not? Some say NO, not healthy, and others see them as supreme medicine. I am not sure yet. And what about fermented foods? Again, some say supreme medicine, and others the opposite. I am making my way through these decisions. I have said NO to soy (except for Bragg). Molten lava cake with ice cream? Well...

And now that I am finding Weston A. Price around every corner (google him) that is turning me back to (carefully raised) meat and dairy. I think I wore out my doctor's patience at my last appointment when I asked him to rate, on a scale of 1 to 10, how important it is to soak nuts and how important it was to include freshly ground flaxseed to my diet. I will carefully work through these decisions myself from now on.

The choices I am making are not about fear of cancer, but rather are motivated by a celebration of life. (I think I want to stick around and enjoy a bit more of it!) I am not fearing cancer. I am embracing it, and thanking it for the huge springboard it gave me for making so many positive changes in my life. In fact my blog, which is called The Vocabulary of Joy, Celebrating the Blessings of Life with Cancer (at julieparker.me) is all about the wonderful, magical blessings that have absolutely poured into my life since my diagnosis September 24th. I recognized from the start that this cancer was a very good thing. And I am not beating myself up for past, uh, fast food, high fructose corn syrup, or for anything else. Whatever I have done got me here, and this is an excellent place to be.

TO TASTE OR NOT TO TASTE
What is interesting about ovarian cancer is that one of the symptoms is loss of appetite. For several months I had to actually force myself to eat. I remember one day I had nothing but a single cup of ginger tea. When I drove past my favorite restaurants — Thai, Indian, Asian restaurants of all sorts, I'd even feel a sort of revulsion. After surgery and a bit of time, my appetite was back and now everything tastes delicious! I am savoring every mouthful. It is almost like I had never really tasted before. Why? Well, I am not sure, but I am eating mindfully, for one thing. I rarely did that before. And I am expressing gratitude more than ever before. I really enjoy sending out appreciation to the sun and the soil and the bees and the beekeepers and the earthworms, the farmers and the grocers and everyone and everything that moved the vegetables from seed to my table.

THANKS!
And I am grateful to the folks at Integrative Family Medicine of Asheville who with their free classes on cooking, healthy budget shopping, growing your own foods, using foods as medicine, and herbal medicine, deeply understand the role of food in healing. I am grateful to my dear friend Debra Roberts (who sent me their way) and who is spreading the word of the supreme importance of bees in supporting our whole food system. (See holybeepress. com) I am grateful too to Laurey Masterton who was another loving bee mama (or a bee-lovin' mama?), who also loved teaching kids about nutrition and who poured her heart into connecting local farmers with local eaters. This is a woman who understood eating as celebration.
So instead of poisoning my body with chemotherapy, I invite all beautiful foods full of life force energy to join with my body's own healing ability and dance. L'chaim!

Illusions, Confusions, and Clarity
MAY 8, 2014

I suppose most of you know this image – look at it one way and it is an old woman – look at it another way and it is a girl. It all depends on how you look at it, right?

Right now I am out of work, out of money, and homeless. Oh yes, and I have cancer. But if I refocus, if I squint a bit and maybe tilt my head, these are the best days of my life!

I am so happy to be back in Asheville, right in the thick of things. It is so quick and easy to get wherever I want to go, and I have started going places! Yes, Julie Parker is making the scene. I am meeting new people and seeing people I had not seen in years. One person I ran into actually thought I was dead! She had heard about the cancer and I had been 'underground' for so long, she actually thought I was pushing up daisies. At a gathering here where I am staying, TWO women in the course of the evening actually said "Oh, YOU'RE Julie Parker!"

There have many things about my life that needed to change and having no work/money/home is forcing them on me. Yes, necessity is the mother of reinvention!

Little Tiny Brooms
MAY 8, 2014

I am halfway through a 21-day cleanse. No meat, dairy, bread, sugar, recreational drugs, alcohol, etc. I have been feeding myself fresh organic veggies, green smoothies, etc. Every morning starts with hot water and lemon like my grandmother used to do. I am snacking on almonds and loving them. Green tea, tulsi tea and dandelion root tea during the day…

I am very curious what my post-cleanse weight will be. Surely I will step off the scales wearing a big smile. I am imagining all my little worker bee cells are busy with tiny brooms, sweeping up debris from years of not-the-best food and drink, and looking for all the

The Vocabulary of Joy

exits. In the meantime, any remaining cancer cells (if there are any) are screaming and crying and gnashing their teeth. "Feed us crap! PLEASE feed us crap! We're dying here! SUGAR! We want sugar! We want sugar! Give us meat! Give us wheat!" No wonder I can't sleep with all that racket going on in my body…
I am worshipping at the altar of my Vitamix (vitamix.com) and rediscovering my love of cooking. Ellen has provided many recipes to get us safely through these three weeks.

We are a group of 32 people, sometimes hanging onto each other for dear life as we ride the waves of our addictions dying off one by one. 21 days of letting go, of forging new habits, of loving our bodies more than we do our cravings. Ellen Kittredge is our ringleader, our nursemaid, our taskmaster, and our inspiration. She gentles us along with encouragement and advice and confidence in our ability to make these changes.

My guess is that I will do this every spring from now on… and that my regular diet will be very close to this. I have always thought that if you fill yourself with enough GOOD food, your body will begin to crave it.

I have so much appreciation for Ellen's vast knowledge and gentle heart, and for Dr. Lewis and Dr. Krisel (with their passion for the well-being of their patients) for sponsoring this cleanse, and for my fellow cleansers and their courage to keep their heads down and keep moving forward through terrain which, for the most of us, is foreign soil. And bless the cancer for forcing me down this path. *"Damn the [cancer cells] – full speed ahead!!"*

Growing a Tumor
MAY 28, 2014
"When your life falls apart, you can either grow or you can grow a tumor. I decided that instead of allowing my body to continue to manifest my stressors physically, it was time to wake up and do

whatever it would take to finally get healthy, inside and out." Lissa Rankin

There are two women who are my sheros: Lissa Rankin and Kris Carr. Kris you can find on crazysexylife.com and kriscarr.com and Lissa at mindovermedicinebook.com and lissarankin.com. They are both about – well, let me think what they are about – taking their health in their own hands. Christiane Northrup says of Lissa Rankin: "Dr. Rankin represents the best of the new generation of young women who are honoring the feminine, embracing our female bodies, and doing so with humor, pleasure, honesty, and a sense of fun." By the way, Lissa has a fun book called *What's Up Down There? Questions You'd Only Ask Your Gynecologist if She Were Your Best Friend.*

Christiane's quote above about Lissa Rankin could apply as well to Kris Carr. Kris was an actress who got cancer and Lissa a doctor who had a pile of illnesses/conditions and an even bigger pile of medications, until they both decided ENOUGH! and turned their lives around, and now are helping other folks take charge and turn themselves around. Well, I am busy turning myself around, taking charge of my own healing.

I think you would enjoy their sites but you might want to wait until you have a bit of time to enjoy them.

Kris has a 40 Day Whole Health Challenge program – the quote above is from that. I am about to dig into it, to see what it is all about. I successfully finished a 21-day cleanse last week and now my doctor wants me totally off all grains for 2 months to see how I feel. I have a new Ayurvedic practitioner – Vishnu Dass – who gave me the sternest lecture yet about getting 100% off ALL forms of sugar. Not that my primary care doctor (PCD) did not make that clear, not that my own reading did not make that clear. I am being challenged right and left, it seems, to step up to the plate and JUST DO IT.

The Vocabulary of Joy

My PCD was telling me on Monday details about how the food industry has so carefully tailored foods for addiction with the perfect balance of fat, salt, and sugar. He said for example, with Doritos, you have to lick your fingers and that gives you yet another 'hit' making you want more. Cheetos too, I guess, even more so. "It's not a fair fight!" he was saying, when we think it is just a failure of our willpower but we are up against huge marketing departments of mega-corporations. That is why it is best to just go completely off processed food.

I have wandered a bit off of the initial concept of growing our tumors. My life fell apart and I grew a tumor. From the beginning I have suspected a strong connection there. Also she writes of the 'pay-off' of illness in getting attention. Hmm. Is my ovarian cancer an attention-seeking behavior? Well, I don't think it was pre-meditated, I really don't, but I admit it has been glorious! Friends, family, nurses, doctors… I had so little contact with people in these last few years and I LOVED being in closer contact with folks when the cancer arrived on the scene. But no, I don't think my head had that in mind when it started growing cancer, but I bet my heart did…

Coming Undone
AUGUST 31, 2014

"For a seed to achieve its greatest expression, it must come completely undone. The shell cracks, its insides come out and everything changes. To someone who doesn't understand growth, it would look like complete destruction."
Cynthia Occelli

I have come completely undone in the last four years. Every aspect of my life unraveled and in the end, my insides came out too – literally. At first I panicked when the ground beneath my feet shook and I began to slide into a deep crevasse as everything I held dear crumbled around me.

Now I am beginning to see signs of growth. Perhaps I am beginning to sprout...

Leaping in with Both Feet
FEBRUARY 9, 2015

Funny thing, I have been out of business cards for my BUSINESS (web design) for quite a while now, but last week I created business cards for The Vocabulary of Joy which isn't even a business! It has become my passion, though, my raison d'etre, at least in this part of my life. I so want to help people move away from fear about cancer, to understand there is so much we can do to heal. The media play up cancer as being so awful, so deadly, it has become the "Disease that must not be named," hence "The Big C". There is so much emphasis on early detection which I feel just engenders fear. OMG do I have cancer yet in this body part, or that one? Or maybe the other one? And if they find something, QUICK!

In Which I We Meet Julie Dumpty

"Have i gone mad?
I'm afraid so, but let me tell you something,
the best people usually are."
Lewis Carroll, Alice in Wonderland

A s I was working on the book this morning, I eyed the pile of papers next to me I was filing (or really, procrastinating filing), and decided to file just file whatever couple of papers my hand fell on, just to get *something* done. I came across this, written at the turn-of-the-century when I was walking through my Dark Night of the Soul. I barely remember writing it, but it made it safely through all 14 moves, so I thought it must be appropriate to include here as it could easily apply to someone with a fresh diagnosis of cancer:

My name is Julie, though it might as well be Alice, for the
Wonderland I have stepped into for the past year. Black became
white, up became down, in became out, nothing became
everything and everything became nothing. The "wonderland" was
anything but wonder-FUL. (READ: Dark Night of the Soul, etc.).

It started, as all good adventures in Wonderland do, by falling
down a very deep hole. I tumbled, flailing, seeing nothing but

darkness and the abyss below. Voices from the sidelines cried "Off with her head!" Maniacal laughter from a B-movie soundtrack echoed as I fell.

Upon reaching the bottom, unlike Alice who stood up with hardly a rumple in her crinoline, I landed with maximum force, impaled on razor-sharp shards of my own making. Julie Dumpty, as it were, now in eggshell-delicate fragments littering the landscape. I journeyed for some time carrying myself in a fishnet bag, losing pieces of myself with every move I made. Ah yes, and then there was the pool of tears! Let me tell you about wading in the pool of tears...

Even once I landed, the ground beneath my feet continued to shift, crumble, and turn to dust. Then one day the Mother whispered "Don't you see? It's happening everywhere! The tremors you feel in your life, your own Richter scale, is but a mirror of me. You are one with me, and we are on this journey together."

And I looked about me with eyes full of tears, and I saw the earth in fragments, broken into pieces by my own tears. And the fragments were beautiful! And I looked in the mirror at my own eggshell form, and I too was beautiful—cracks, tears, and all.

"You are becoming whole." she whispered. "But first you must come apart. You must let go of everything you believe in, everything you cherish. It is time, my dear one, to come unglued!"

And I heard her, and I understood.

And our dance continued, and my lessons continued. Having lost, in the past year, the two people I cherish most on earth, I lay exhausted, wounded, on the extraordinarily beautiful spot the universe kindly led me to. It was a spot of such beauty that I began a line of greeting cards from photos taken from my own hill, from the 360 degrees surrounding me.

The Vocabulary of Joy

*And then one day my landlady came and told me I had to move.
The land beneath my feet shook with fierce intensity as I faced
the prospect of literally losing the land beneath my feet—and the
source and muse for my new work. Another abyss, another pool of
tears. This time I only allowed myself to fall for 24 hours, and then
I landed with a thud. I stood up, dusted myself off, and that very
day found a wonderful new place. Even more beautiful, exactly
matching what I value, and... exactly the same rent!*

*My one concern was the nature of the land. I had been for a year
on a hill surrounded with distant views of great beauty in all
directions: soft rolling hills, sunrise, sunset, horses, cows, goats!*

*The new place was in its own cove, the only distant view being
a narrow slice straight ahead. Well yes, it did have a stream, a
house in my favorite style, two porches and a deck, lush gardens
including my favorite—peonies; a barn, a chicken coop, a garage,
a guest house, an organic garden, etcetera, but I still wasn't sure
it was the place for me, with only one narrow, distant view! So I
asked the Mother for a sign that this was the place for me. Then I
went back over to the new place (where my landlords lived at the
time) ready to give them my deposit should I decide it was a go,
and my landlady said "I want to show you what I got in the mail
yesterday." And she brought into the room a plain white sheet of
paper, folded in half and taped—a cheap flyer. And stuck to her
flyer, as sometimes happens with bulk mail, was another person's
flyer—mine! Addressed to me, at my old address, this flyer was
delivered to my new mailbox! A clear sign, delivered in my mailbox
yet, with the universe's marvelous sense of humor!*

*And now while I wait the few weeks until my move, the Mother
and I whisper daily, like schoolgirls. She taps me on the shoulder
while I am at my computer in the early morning saying "Quick!
Look outside!" and I fly with my camera to catch another
spectacular sunrise just outside my window. Then I come in and
slip the image onto my computer and begin to co-create with the*

Celebrating the Blessings of Life with Cancer

Mother... I shatter and shift and reconfigure what I have just seen, creating kaleidoscopes, even while she continues to shift the sunrise out my window. They are mandalas from bits and pieces of the digital image. The sun and sky are still in their glory, still muse to my mandalas, being created minutes from the moment the image was taken. And sometimes the Mother sends one of my dogs to me, a cold nose saying "Quick! Look at the late afternoon light on the barns!" Or two dog noses saying "Look at that giant rainbow!"

And now in my own life, when the ground begins to quake, I know it is the Mother, and I smile. Okay, sometimes I also whimper a bit. This is, after all, a story of transformation, but not quite full-blown enlightenment. Perhaps in my next chapter?

Planting Groundhogs

Groundhogs aren't faring very well in my neck of the woods these days. Groundhog corpses are appearing here and there in my yard, aided and abetted, I suspect, by my dogs Cricket and Anna. I thanked them for their gifts to me—last year I found a large rabbit head in my long dark hallway—and explained I'd prefer they let all the little animals live in peace. Tails wagged and tongues lolled, and all I got was empty promises.

A particularly large ex-groundhog made its appearance one day when I was finding even the simplest of tasks overwhelming. I put off dealing with the body. My friend Irv suggested picking it up with a shovel and throwing it onto the roof of the chicken coop, where it would be taken care of by the flesh-eating birds and out of the reach of the dogs. (Irv has two dogs of his own, and apparently this technique works well for him).

I was doubtful that I could master the technique of groundhog slinging. Visions of groundhog corpses falling back onto my head persuaded me to procrastinate a bit longer. Have you ever found that if you put something off long enough, you don't have to deal with it at all? At times, procrastination has been my Primary Spiritual Practice.

Stepping outside one morning a few weeks later, I found the groundhog was no more. Perhaps it has ascended, I thought,

Celebrating the Blessings of Life with Cancer

hopefully, relieved and grateful that I no longer had to deal with it. It wasn't until the next morning when my eyes wandered up to one of the flowerbeds that I saw where the groundhog had found his final resting place. Approaching the body gingerly, I saw it was bloated and full of maggots. Euw, euw! Euw. I decided the wisest course of action was to cover it with a cardboard box and procrastinate some more. After all, slinging maggot-infested groundhog corpses onto the roofs of chicken coops is no one's idea of a good time (with the possible exception of Irv!)

At this point I adopted a philosophical attitude towards the whole affair. I blessed the maggots, thanked them for doing their job, and wished them Godspeed. This is the natural cycle of life, and all quite appropriate, I decided. And I was in no hurry to peek under the cardboard box again.

But one morning as I stepped into the garden, I found the cardboard box was gone, and where it had been was a bit of fur, a few bones, and what looked like the richest, blackest soil I had ever seen. Yes! This is good, I thought. And procrastination having worked so well for me to this point, I still took no action.

A week or so later my cousin Katherine and her husband Jim were visiting. Katherine was helping me plant several flats of impatiens a friend had given me. I'd suggested she plant them anywhere on the little hill of tiered flowerbeds behind my house, while I continued to focus on the speck of garden by my back door. Then we cleaned up, had dinner, and they left the next morning.

That afternoon I looked to see exactly what she had done, and I found she had planted most of the impatiens smack dab in the middle of the groundhog!

It wasn't until a few weeks later that I discovered The Moral of the Story. Stepping out into the garden one morning, I noticed that the flowers planted in the groundhog were thick and luscious and radiant in the morning sun; the impatiens in the flowerbed only inches away were as puny as others were fine.

The proverbial light bulb went off immediately and I saw the dark, ugly, maggot-infested terrain I had passed through the previous year was truly a gift, truly that which was the rich, fertile soil for my own blossoming.

Mind you, I have always stubbornly resisted this "suffering is good for you" stuff. "You have to know the pain to feel the joy." Phooey. Who makes up this stuff, anyway? But I am coming to believe that it is just possible that a Dark Night of the Soul can be a good thing. Just what the doctor ordered, actually. Is it possible that what looks like the maggot-infested corpse of my life is really compost for my own metamorphosis? The evidence is still unfolding. I'll get back to you on this.

First published in WNC WOMAN magazine, January 2002

I Lost My Mother in the Backseat of My Car

I lost my mother in the back seat of my car.

She isn't far, you see. I could just reach her, I'm sure, if I knew where to look.

I lost my mother in the back seat of my car.
My car—full of the flotsam and jetsam of my life—is the last stronghold of the days of darkness.

I lost my mother in the back seat of my car.
She's back there somewhere. I am afraid to look.

I lost my mother in the back seat of my car.
She was a small woman, you know, who grew smaller as she aged.
She left this life in ounces.

I lost my mother in the back seat of my car.
We spent her last day together, the two of us.
I sat beside her while she was interviewing angels.

I lost my mother in the back seat of my car.
She was my mother, my best friend—and then she was dust.

I Lost My Mother in the Backseat of My Car

I lost my mother in the back seat of my car.
It was like this: I was moving—again. Feeling displaced. Rootless.
So rootless that this time I was even carrying with me the roots of
my own flesh.

I lost my mother in the back seat of my car.
She was riding in the back seat in a small box, and the box got
lost, you know. There was so much to sort through back there—so
much I didn't want to see!

I lost my mother in the back seat of my car.
It was really her car, is the thing. I bought it from her.
I gave her four quarters.
You know that little table that slides across the hospital bed?
I laid them there, one by one. Just something to make it legal.
Four quarters for a whole car! Four quarters make a whole.
Four quarters for a whole car, for a whole life . . .
Four quarters that said I would leave with the car, and the wallet,
and the keys, and the glasses, and the slippers, and everything that
was of "substance" in her life. I'd even leave with the four quarters.
Those four quarters were the first time we looked into each other's
eyes and said, "Well, this is it, I guess."

I lost my mother in the back seat of my car.
She kept saying, "I'm not afraid to die, you know—I'm just not
packed yet."
The doctors grinned. She charmed them all, even with her last
breaths.

I lost my mother in the back seat of my car.
I'd promised her to clean it up and return it after my last move,
just weeks before she, uh, before she . . .

But I'd been too busy, watching her die. She never got it back. I
never cleaned it up. And then she got lost in it.
Lost in the jumble of fear and pain that rode around in the back

Celebrating the Blessings of Life with Cancer   169

seat in the guise of stacks and boxes and bags and papers and
books and unidentifiable crap that I could not budge.
And cannot budge today, almost three years later.
It's two moves later, and there is still unidentifiable crap
in the back of my car.

I lost my mother in the back seat of my car.
I wonder if she would see the humor in that?
She had such a sense of humor. Until her last breath. I think she
would have laughed. And then been pissed.
And then laughed some more.

I lost my mother in the back seat of my car.
I finally found her, you know. Grateful that I was saved from the
fate of being some kind of monstrous daughter who'd lose her
mother in the rubble of her own despair.

And now I've lost my mother somewhere in my house.
She isn't far, I'm sure. I could just reach her . . . if I knew where to
look.

First published in WNC WOMAN magazine, May 2003

The Vocabulary of Joy

In Which We Meet Another Julie

"Cancer is not the enemy; it is the messenger. Much like a
headache can indicate vision challenges, or poor diet, or addiction.
It alerts me to the fact that something isn't right in my body. Is it
my hormones? My metabolism? My blood? My diet? My lifestyle?
Cancer isn't mysterious or spontaneous. It has a purpose."
Julie Khindria

The following showed up this morning on Facebook—a kindred
spirit also named Julie. She has kindly given me permission to
include this in my book and I am so aligned with what she is
saying, this whole chapter is her post. Thank you Julie for sharing
this with us!

'd like to express my heart, and share my views on Cancer, in an
effort to create better understanding and garner more support
surrounding my circumstance...

First, I don't view Cancer as a disease. Cancer is a *symptom*
of underlying and overlooked dis-ease. It's is the symptom of
systemic imbalance.

Second, Cancer is not the enemy; it is the messenger. Much
like a headache can indicate vision challenges, or poor diet, or
addiction. It alerts me to the fact that something isn't right in my
body. Is it my hormones? My metabolism? My blood? My diet? My

lifestyle? Cancer isn't mysterious or spontaneous. It has a purpose. My job is to figure it out. I need to decode the messages, identify the short circuits and imbalances.

I am a puzzle with many pieces, each with its own unique design, place, and purpose. Out of place, the picture grows distorted. And without that piece, the picture simply ceases to exist. When given the pieces—the tools—our bodies are miraculous little machines. And the earth, nature, is miraculous in its own right—perfectly balanced and perfectly equipped. My body is part of that perfect balance. The natural state of the human form is homeostasis. Our natural state is health. We are designed to heal. Our immune systems are powerhouses that prepare us for battle all day, every day. But for some, these powerhouses fall a bit short.

Approximately 7% of all cancers are "genetic," meaning that there is a history of Cancer, a genetic mutation, or a specific gene that is present in multiple generations of a single lineage. The rest (93%) are diet, lifestyle, and environment related. That means they can be prevented, controlled, and reversed, in theory, IF we heed the messengers and figure out what's missing. What's wrong. What did we do and what can we do? And that's where I am. I'm asking my body what it needs to heal. I'm listening to my intuition. And I'm reading and researching like it's my six-figure job (if I make it out of this alive, it *will* be!).

So if I don't seem scared enough, or like I don't understand the weight of the situation, or if it seems I should be jumping on every available standard treatment they offer, but I'm dragging my feet and being stubborn, know that I am not ignoring or defying my doctors; I'm not in denial; I'm not naïve; and I'm not rejecting modern medicine; I am listening to and respecting my body, which knows better than anyone what it's doing, and how to re-establish balance within, with the help of diligent research, CAM therapies, and faith that everything will be as it should be.

The Vocabulary of Joy

ACKNOWLEDGMENTS

Whitman Bolles—I have to put you right up at the top, even though you are the most recent addition to the pantheon of people I deeply appreciate. Everybody—meet my editor, Whitman. Lordy, did he use both carrot and stick to prod, cajole, and inspire me to dig deeper, and to write a much more authentic (if way-more-revealing-than-I-planned-to) book.

Julia Nooe—you have been noodging me to write my story for a long time. Now here it is—you can quit noodging! And thank you by the way. Also for putting up with me in my "I don't know and I don't care" times.

Debra Roberts—you always keeps my eyes focused on my Sacred Next. Thank you for connecting me with Whitman, and with Brian. What a blessing you are in my life! What would I do without you?

Katherine and Jim Ingram—you have shown abiding love and kindness to me and support in so many ways in my cancer journey and in my life. I treasure you both!

Thanks also to **Chad Krisel, MD**, my secondary primary care doctor, whose warmth and caring and heartfelt hugs are a superb example of Lissa Rankin's words about the healing power of the doctor's loving kindness. (And much appreciation to the whole cast and crew at **IFMA**!)

Priestley Ford, you have been there for me again and again in so many ways. I won't mention the diaper incident. Oh wait—I guess I did.

Thank you **Doris Thrift** for your friendship since what seems like the beginning of time, and for your support in the lean and scary years. And for the email in the hospital!

Herb and Karen Bandy, I love it when y'all make your annual pilgrimage from the Bunny Planet! And thank you for all your loving support of my healing in between. And for using your super powers on my behalf...

T, wow! You were so dear for driving me to my nephrectomy surgery and for sitting by my side all that first night and half the next day and for all you have done since. And for standing by my side on Anna's last day.

Matthew Miroslav Kabat, it knocks my socks off that you and Brian materialize on my roof each Thursday and open up a whole new world to us. I sit at your feet in awe.

Laura and Gilles Lefevre, I am so happy you stepped into my life and I thank you for all your kindnesses on this leg of my journey.

Helen (and Pete) McCloskey, I thank you for your generous support and for the literal fruit of your labors—and for your critter stories. Helen, I am so happy you resurfaced in my life!

Barbara Bouse Bielinski, you were the very first to step forward with an investment in this work... I appreciate your trust in what I was doing and all your other kindesses.

Rebecca Word and **Marianne Mitchell** for the gift of your skills and for waiting so long for the article!

Sandra Newes, PhD, thanks for helping me keep my head screwed on straight, and for always 'inviting me' to one thing or the other. And for some really good words!

Kathe McCleave, you came in right under the wire to cheer me on, be a partner in crime, and help in so many ways.

Diane Van Helden, **Antiga**, and **Christopher Mello**: you so kindly took me in when I was about to move into my car! I am so deeply grateful.

Linda McLean, a great big thanks for Battery Park! (Thank heavens I *finally* listened!)

Alla Renee Bozarth: I am indebted to you for generously allowing me to include *Bakerwoman God* and **Judyth Hill** for *Wage Peace*. Both of these poems move me deeply and so reflect my healing process.

Maharishi Mahesh Yogi, you taught me *Yogastah Kuru Karmani* - (established in being, perform action) which has been the basis of my life since 1972 and has been my 'bridge over troubled waters' ever since.

Thanks and abiding love to my mother, **Irma Parker**, for your splendid example of how to leave with grace, dignity, and humor. One day I hope to follow in your footsteps. (Save me a seat!)

Thanks to **Joseph Brown and The Carla Rose Foundation** (thecarlarosefoundation.org) the only non-profit providing financial support for people wanting to heal cancer naturally. Thanks to **Sara Laws and The Hope Chest for Women** (hopechestforwomen.org) that provides support for women with breast and gynecologic cancers in Western North Carolina, and **Kathy Haney** and **Casting for Hope** (castingforhope. org) attending to the financial, emotional, and spiritual needs of women living with ovarian and gynecological cancers in Western North Carolina. I appreciate you all so much!

Lisa, Brian, and Diane: I have such love, respect, and appreciation/ admiration for the three of you! Words can't begin to express my gratitude for your rôles in my healing, so I just had to dedicate the whole book to you...

P.S. I am told it is not appropriate to use **bold** in publishing, but really, how could I do any less?

AFTERWORD

On page two of this book, I wrote "... right here at the beginning I should make it clear why I am writing this book, but the truth is, I just know I need to write it. The *why* of it is unraveling as I write."

Well, here we are at the end of the book and it has pretty much unraveled, though in a way I never expected. I started off all bouncy, tralala, happy to be doing so well and wanting to share what I had learned on the journey. The more I wrote, the more I understood my own cancer journey and my own journey as Julie Savage Parker. I had no idea the book would end up being so intensely personal, so standing-naked-in-the-spotlight.

I don't pretend to have all the answers to healing cancer naturally—I doubt I have half the answers! But at least now I know the right questions...

Susan Statham tells us 'Your life is your story. Write well. Edit often.' By writing my story, or this segment of my story, I have realized this book was not really for you—it was for me! Thank you for joining me in the dance.

ABOUT THE AUTHOR

You could say Julie's writing career started when she was the assistant editor of her high school literary magazine, then languished in the background of her life while she was pursuing other interests. She rekindled her love for the written word in 2002 when she founded a regional women's literary magazine and became a grown-up publisher/editor. Now she has discovered a passion for writing as a tool for healing. She inherited her love for the written word (and her sense of humor) from her mother.

She earned a BFA (Bachelor of Fine Arts) in painting from East Carolina University, and an MS from Gallaudet University where all her classes were in sign language. She almost earned her PhD at The Union Institute (it's a long story).

After living in places ranging from Virginia (her point of origin) to Libya, Morocco (Casablanca, actually), Germany, Paris, and a whole slew of other places, she finally landed in Asheville, right in the heart of the beautiful mountains of Western North Carolina, where she thinks she will probably stay.

The Vocabulary of Joy

The Vocabulary of Joy